HEAVEN, IRON AND I

THE RON MARTINELLI STORY

HEAVEN, IRON AND I
THE RON MARTINELLI STORY

by

Ron Zuccaro

Tribute House Publishing
Macomb County, Michigan

www.tributehousepublishing.com

ISBN 978-0-615-41751-6 *(hardcover)*
ISBN 978-0-615-41751-6 *(paperback)*

Book design by Rose Island Bookworks
Monument photos by Tim Ainsworth

Manufactured in the United States of America

This book is dedicated to
my Lord and Savior, Jesus Christ.
To all the friends I served with in combat,
the United States Military, especially
the U.S.M.C., U.S. Army,
and U.S. Navy of which I served.
My mother and father,
Elaine Zuccaro, Ann Zuccaro, Chris Pozios,
my three sons Ron, Tom and Joey,
my grandsons,
Richie, Tom Tom, Ronnie, Michael and Anthony,
and my great grandsons,
Tom Tom Tom and Angelo.

1-27-17

To Tom

Best of Luck

Your Friend

SEMPER FI

Table of Contents

Preface

I'm Ron Zuccaro a.k.a. Ron Martinelli and this is my story. The challenging times of my life. The Vietnam War and how a truck ran out of control and ran me through the brick wall of a cleaners and surgeons told me I wouldn't walk again. How I opened a gambling casino to help with my financial hardships and how I wrestled as a professional all over the country before my accident and made a comeback, against all odds, to win the championship and how I dealt with all the devastation and obstacles.

I could not have come through it without my Father in Heaven. He never left me. I'm reminded of the poem Footsteps in the Sand and Jesus said "When you only saw one set of footprints, that's when I carried you. Well, He carried me a lot.

This book is about hope, perseverance, love, loyalty, discipline and training. All these things taught to me by my mother, father and the U.S.M.C. in boot camp, and the U.S. Army, and faith in Jesus Christ my Savior. I always turn to Him, believe in and talk to Him. I pray daily and talk to Him like I would talk to my earthly father. I thank God every day that He chose me to be born, the son of that lovely lady, my mother, the Saint. Christ brought me back from a violent and vicious war. He brought peace to my heart and soul. He gave me a wonderful family, three sons, five grandsons and two great grandsons.

My Lord brought me through quadruple by-pass, prostate cancer, and more health issues brought on by Agent Orange. He guided me through the war, the devastating sights of the horror of war, and the death of so many friends.

I will always believe that we won the Vietnam War on the battlefield. They lost one and a half million VC and North Vietnamese, we lost 58,000, and don't get me wrong, one American is too many. We would have lost far less if Washington D.C. had not played politics allowing Charlie sanctuary and continued bombing Hi Phong Harbour, North Hanoi and the Ho Chi Minh Trail. No one defeated us in combat. Nobody, and I emphasize NOBODY. The honor, courage and valor of the American Military shined brightly. I will defend our troops until God takes my last breath. Let no one taint the actions or honor of my brave buddies. This book is a tribute to all the brave Vets and the Living God, Jesus Christ.

Acknowledgements

To Jane Walendzik for typing the manuscript, getting it into digital format and showing me how to get a copyright. To Tim Ainsworth for taking pictures of the memorial and to Susan Leonard for designing, guiding me through and giving me all her time and advice. She did so much to get this book off the ground. I can't thank her enough. To Doreen at Detroit Arms LLC for putting together the web site and to Dion and Larry Evans also at Detroit Arms. To Bill Stroud with who I joined the U.S.M.C. and one of my best friends since I was in school. To William Miller, Lawyer Jones, James Julien, Wallace Alport and Donald McIntosh. To Sr. Vice Commandant Lennie Brooks, my friend Bulldog and all the guys at Belcher-Lane, Marine Corp League, Port Huron, Detachment 146. Semper Fi. To The American Legion, The Veterans of Foreign War, The Disabled American Veterans, Vietnam Veterans of America, and all branches of the U.S. Military To the Nurses and Doctors of Vietnam who saved many lives, to the buddies I served with in peace and war, and to all the men and women who have ever served since the Revolutionary War. And, a special tribute to all those that made the ultimate sacrifice.

Footprints in the Sand

One night I dreamed I was walking
along the beach with the Lord.
Many scenes from my life flashed across the sky.
In each scene I noticed footprints in the sand.
Sometimes there were two sets of footprints,
other times there were one set of footprints.

This bothered me because I noticed
that during the low periods of my life,
when I was suffering from
anguish, sorrow or defeat,
I could see only one set of footprints.

So I said to the Lord,
"You promised me Lord,
that if I followed you,
you would walk with me always.
But I have noticed that during
the most trying periods of my life
there have only been one
set of footprints in the sand.
Why, when I needed you most,
you have not been there for me?"

The Lord replied,
"The times when you have
seen only one set of footprints,
is when I carried you."

Mary Stevenson

The Accident

February 17, 1976. I was at the dry cleaners in Fraser, Michigan to pick up my white suit and dress clothes. I had a wrestling match for the heavy weight championship of the world with the current N.W.A. Champ. It was twelve noon. The proprietor said my cleaning wasn't ready and to come back in a couple hours.

I went home to get my suitcases packed. I had a plane to catch at Detroit Metro Airport at 8pm flying to Miami. The match was the next day at the convention center. I was to arrive in Miami at 10:20pm that night and had reservations at the Holiday Inn at 22nd and Collins in South Beach. All I had to do is go back to the cleaners to pick up the dry cleaning, get something to eat, shower and drive to the airport.

I went back to the cleaners, it was 1:40pm. I picked up my clothes, put them over my left shoulder holding onto the hangers and walked toward the door to go outside. There was a woman holding a baby in front of me. I followed behind her. At that moment I saw a truck racing out of con-

1

trol headed right at the woman with her baby. I dropped my clothes. My mind was racing. There was no time to think, I reacted. I shoved the woman with the baby to the side of the building out of the way. I shoved her hard then put out my arms to hold back the truck. I braced my right leg against the wall, knowing that no man is strong enough to stop a truck out of control but I had no other choice than to try. I was strong for a second, then the wall gave in. I was strong enough not to get splattered.

I was laying in brick rubble on the floor inside the cleaners, my legs were twisted. The truck was on top of me. The axle of the truck was on top of the rubble, the tires still spinning. Exhaust from the truck was choking me and my legs hurt so bad. The plate glass window had broken and cut my stomach. I felt glass in my leg and in my left ear. Pain, so much pain. I looked down at my legs and saw my toes facing down. My leg was completely twisted, the femur sticking out of my pant leg and blood flowing from my body.

I started to hear loud sirens and people screaming. Everything happened so fast. It was all madness, pain, and confusion. My body crushed. I heard a cop yell out. People screamed "He's going to die, the truck crushed him, he will never make it, no one could have survived that."

The cop leaned down, looked under the truck and asked what he could do for me. Did I need something to bite down on, something to help the pain? I asked him to turn off the engine in the truck, I was getting affixiated. I thought I was dying. I looked up and saw the clock in the cleaners, it was 2 o'clock. I had to make it. I had two little boys at home. I made it through the war and I refused to go like this.

I saw strobe lights flashing and all kinds of chaos. The Fire Department arrived. They got me out from under the truck and the paramedics loaded me into the ambulance. They told me to hold on, they would get me to a hospital. I asked them to take me to Mount Clemens General.

I could hear the sirens racing me through the streets. They hooked me up to an IV and got me to the hospital where nurses and doctors were waiting. I heard the paramedic tell them I was in bad shape. They rushed me into surgery and the lights went out.

. . .

I woke up in the Intensive Care Unit with nurses and doctors around me. The pain was excruciating. They gave me a shot of Demerol and I went to sleep. Intensive care would be my home for the next ten days.

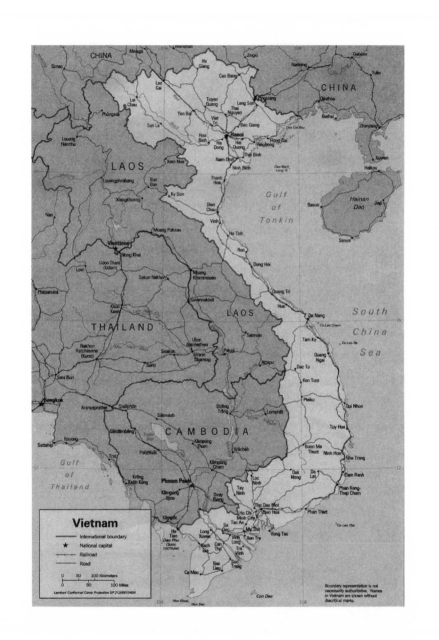

Vietnam

- International boundary
- ★ National capital
- Railroad
- Road

Lambert Conformal Conic Projection SP 21;26N;104;0N

Flashback One

I'm in Pleiku in the Central Highlands of Vietnam. My infantry unit is lined up loading on gunships. Huey's going to hit a hot landing zone (LZ). We get loaded and the choppers take off for the LZ. My stomach feels like it's in my mouth. I'm scared but I've been trained well and my Lord is at my side. He's given me comfort all my life.

We get to the LZ and the North Vietnamese are shooting at our choppers. We're taking on a lot of machine gun fire and bullets are ripping through the chopper. There is no time to think and the adrenaline is pumping. I pray for God to protect me and ask him to please let me see my two baby boys again.

The chopper hovers over elephant grass 7 or 8 feet off the ground. We're under fire. We jump but the chopper is vulnerable. I hit the ground hard. The M-16 I carry hit me in the face. I run to take a position, diving to the ground, bullets hitting all around me. I fire back from a shallow hole where there are ants crawling all over me. I can't get out. The ants are biting me and I can't get out without getting shot. My friend yells, "Ron you've been shot, you need a medic." I yell back, "I only have a bloody nose from the M-16 hitting my face when I jumped." I keep firing. Choppers are crashing to the ground. The landscape looks like a junkyard. People are screaming in pain and dying. I've landed in hell.

A dustoff evacuation helicopter drops down to get our wounded out. We help load the litters into the chopper. The pilots try to get some lift off the ground but Charlie is jumping onto the landing skids. We shoot Charlie off the skids so they can get out.

We form a perimeter defense but our 1st platoon is getting over run by human wave attacks. There are several choppers down. The fight goes on for hours.

I can hear my friends yelling that they're wounded, saying that they're freezing. It's 116° in the jungle. They're cold because they're bleeding to death and I don't know how to help them. There is blood all over. Pain, anguish, bodies scattered everywhere.

I'm caught in a nightmare wondering when it will end. I want to vomit but I don't have time. I pray, Lord let the hell end. It seems like it will never end. We can't shoot them fast enough. Bodies are falling all over us. Holy terror. My fatigues are covered with blood, my hands and face. The awful smell of blood.

Intensive Care

I had a flashback to the war. I woke up in intensive care soaked with sweat. The pain was overwhelming. It shot through my foot and ankle like bolts of lightning. The doctor came in to give me the bad news. The peroneal nerve in my leg had been severed in the accident, I would never walk again.

I refused to listen. This couldn't be happening. I prayed to God for strength. Jesus had always been at my side. He would help me get through this. All things are possible with Jesus. I don't deserve his help but he would never leave me.

I was going to prove this doctor wrong. I had been through worse. I had been to hell and I wasn't going to let this beat me. The North Vietnamese couldn't beat me and this accident wouldn't either as long as I had my Father, my Lord, my God with me. If it was his will I would make it through this. No man or mountain could stop me.

I finally got the shot and the pain started to ease off. My boys and family came in to visit for a few minutes. My son Ron was 14 and Tom was 12. I was so happy after their visit. I fell back to sleep.

Flashback Two

I'm in the jungle walking rear guard with my squad strategically 15 meters apart and counting paces. I have a shoelace hanging from my pistol belt. I tie a knot in the shoelace every so many paces so I know how many kilometers we've gone.

We have our machetes out cutting a trail through the jungle. We can't use an established trail because Charlie could wait and ambush us on our way out. All of a sudden I hear a noise. My eyes are wide trying to see what it is. I look at my feet for snakes or a bamboo pit viper. If you get bit by a viper, you're dead. Cobras are also highly poisonous and deadly. Maybe it's a tiger. My heart is pounding, I'm afraid it's Charlie.

I hear a snort. I turn to see a wild boar looking right at me, hitting his hoof on the ground. If the boar makes a move to charge his tusk will gouge me to death. Oh God, be with me. I back up slowly with my M-16 pointed at him. I have two magazines taped together. Even if I put 20 rounds in him he can still get me before he dies. I keep backing up.

He doesn't charge, he snorts and goes in a different direction. I'm so relieved.

. . .

We've been on patrol for hours. We're lost. Our squad leader followed the river bed instead of checking his compass. We soon discover we're in Cambodia, right in the middle of a North Vietnamese Army (N.V.A.) staging area. It's nightfall and dark in the jungle. We hide in the high elephant grass, the North Vietnamese are all around us.

My heart is pounding so hard and I wonder if I'll ever see my little boys again. I'm sure they can hear me breathing. Oh Lord, please get me out of this. I hear their voices. They're so close I can smell them. I'm afraid they're going to step on me. All I can do is pray. Can't burp, can't slap a mosquito, can't sneeze, can't scratch. Pray. My stomach is sick and my mind is racing. My little boys, please Lord, they need me. If I die now I'll never know what they look like. I'll never play ball with them. Please, help me Lord.

I carry a coin in my pocket that was a gift from my mother. The coin reads "God grant me the serenity to accept the things I cannot change, change the things I can, and have the wisdom to know the difference." I hold it to my heart and squeeze. It gives me comfort.

We hide in the daylight by camouflaging ourselves. At night we crawl to get some distance from the enemy. I pray if I don't make it the Lord will help me overcome my fears. I ask for the courage to die with my friends and to be a loyal trooper, to let my family know that I wouldn't run and to watch over them.

. . .

It's been three days and we are still making our way back to the Unit. We come up to a river and we're vulnerable as we cross over when Charlie ambushes and opens up gunfire. Bullets are flying. I'm on top of some boulders in the river with grenades hitting all around. All hell has broken loose. Screaming death everywhere. It's madness. I'm firing back. Bullets are hitting in the water next to me. I go under the water and start treading, trying to get a pocket of air under my helmet so I can breath.

Suddenly it's over as quick as it began. Charlie disengages. It lasted only minutes but it seemed like an eternity. Five of my buddies are dead in the river, two are wounded, five of us are okay. Fourteen N.V.A. dead and I don't know how many wounded. The river is red with blood. I'm soaked with water, blood and mud. My body is shaking, my head is beating like a base drum and my chest feels like it's about to explode. How much longer can I live? ...hours? ...minutes? It's constantly on my mind. Seven of us make it back to our Unit after three terror filled days.

Realization

I woke up in intensive care soaked with sweat, tears running down my cheeks. I was relieved to find myself in the hospital with a broken body rather than the war zone. Then I came to the realization that I couldn't get out of bed on my own and that I may never walk again.

I called for the nurse to give me medication for the pain. She said it was too soon, I had to wait for two more hours. I didn't think I could make it. All I could do was wait in pain and watch the clock and count the minutes. It seemed like days. The pain was awful. Finally the nurse came in, gave me a shot of Demerol and I fell back to sleep.

Flashback Three

Back in Vietnam. It's midnight and my infantry company is pulling perimeter guard around a battery of 105 Howitzers. Charlie usually hits with a large force between 10p.m. and 3a.m. under cover of darkness. Once he attacks the fight is on. They can outnumber us 8 to 1 then retreat back to their sanctuary in Cambodia. Under the cover of darkness we are not allowed to pursue, use artillery or call in air strikes. Our leaders in Washington D.C. have screwy rules of engagement.

Three of us are in a bunker manned with a M-60 machine gun. We each have an M-16 and four grenades, two on each ammo pouch, for a total of twelve grenades. Bandoleers of ammo with plenty of 7.62 ammo for our M-16's. Two magazines taped together, we have plenty of magazines. Out in front of our position is a claymore mine. 105 Howitzers fire illuminated rounds with concentration firing around the perimeter to light up the area because it's so dark we can't see 15 feet in front of us.

All of a sudden we've got incoming mortar rounds.

Thoot-Thoot. Explosions light up the midnight sky. Screaming North Vietnamese charge in human wave attacks firing AK-47's and throwing grenades. Our line opens up fire. My mind is racing.

Charlie breaks through our 2nd platoon and gets inside the perimeter. They throw a white phosphorus grenade inside the ammo hootch. Over 500 rounds of 105 Howitzer rounds explode with shrapnel flying everywhere. The night sky is lit up. People are screaming and bodies fall all over. They take our #6 Howitzer and fire directly at the #5 gun. They miss. Our #5 gun fires back with a canister round. It's loaded with hundreds of flechette that kill Charlie and we're able to get the #6 gun back.

Artillery men are fighting in hand to hand combat. Screaming, cursing, wild madness with no end in sight. Charlie is hopped up on opium and keeps charging. We have no time to even change machine gun barrels. They're so hot they glow in the dark.

We're getting hit with so many human wave attacks we have to call in for Napalm air strikes on our own position. The planes come dropping napalm which creates a huge firestorm, like a rolling wall of fire. It's like being in the pits of hell. The North Vietnamese are on fire and start running back up the hill. The battle rages on a few more hours but it feels like forever.

The enemy has to disengage. Inhumane acts brought back humanity and the enemy lost. He wanted to completely annihilate us but he was not to have his feast on us this time. I'm overcome with a great feeling of relief and joy that this violent fight is coming to an end and I've been spared. The comfort lasts only briefly.

As I start to look around I see bodies everywhere, bodies missing arms and legs. Downed helicopters. The smell of burnt flesh is unforgettable. Many of my friends are dead. One of my bunker buddies is dead, shot through the head. One of my best friends has the back of his head taken off from shrapnel. His eyes are spinning. Vomit all over him. I grab him up in my arms and cradle him trying to put the pieces of his skull back. Please no, not him. I'm balling like a baby begging God to help me make him okay. I have to get him well. I have to.

We've been through everything together. At war you become closer with your buddy than your own brother. We share love, hardship and our innermost feelings. I love my buddies and this one is close to my heart. I'll never forget. Nothing will ever erase it.

My Lord says, "Love your enemies and pray for those who persecute you," but I feel so much hate for Charlie. The sight of their dead makes me feel good. My mind, heart, and body are so confused. It's hard not to go crazy. I'm in a world of evil and I turn to Him to end my pain. Without Him I would be a mad man but I wonder how much more I can take. I pray for answers. I cry until I can't cry anymore. I'm exhausted, my heart is empty and broken but I've got to go on.

Refuse to Believe

I woke up again terrorized in sweat and tears. I found out I'd been in intensive care for 10 days. The doctor told me I would be moved to a regular room in a few hours. He says how fortunate I am to be alive, to be thankful and to accept that I won't walk again. The sooner I accept that fact, he said, and learn how to live with it the better off I'd be. I needed to learn a new way to live with my disability. It would take therapy, both physical and mental.

I got angry listening to him. I told him I didn't accept it and the only therapy I needed would be physical. I didn't need a psychiatrist because my mind was strong. I would never give up. Not only would I walk, I'd wrestle again, no matter how long it took.

I was determined to make him eat his words. I had faith in God and I had faith in myself. I refused to accept anything negative. I didn't want to hear any more that he had to say if he didn't stop the negativity. I wanted a different doctor. He seemed disgusted with me. As he left the room he turned and said, "I hope it turns out for you. I don't want you to have false hopes."

I laid there and prayed to God. I've turned to Him ever since I was a child. Whenever I needed Him I talked to Him. He was, and will always be, my best friend.

There was one time when I was a little boy and I wanted a puppy dog. My dad said no. If my dad said no he meant it, there was no use asking him again. I prayed for 2 or 3 days. Finally my Lord changed my dad's heart. It was a miracle. In high school when I played baseball I prayed. Football, he would always come through for me. I had no reason to doubt my Lord. I knew hard work and faith would get me through this. I expected my miracle.

They moved me out of intensive care to a private room. I was in a lot of pain and scared. The pain was unbearable. I felt like a drug addict as I watched the clock. I needed my shot. Finally the nurse came in to give me another shot and I fell back to sleep.

Flashback Four

We're getting mortar rounds raining down on us. My platoon is coming in from patrol. It's about an hour before dark, a little early for Charlie to attack. We've got about 30 yards to go before we're inside the perimeter. My buddy and I are running to get to a bunker. He's a Platoon Sergeant, 44 years old. Being 19 years younger I have a couple of steps on him. I made it. He's two steps behind. A mortar explodes and I hear him yell. Shrapnel got him in the groin. He fell outside the bunker. I pull him inside, he's bleeding profusely and only semi conscious. I hold him. He let out a sigh I know he's gone.

. . .

He was my friend. We were stationed together in 1961 during the Cuban Missile Crisis. I was a SGT E-5 and he was a SFC E-7. We were ready to make an amphibious landing when President Kennedy reached an agreement with Khrushchev of Russia and we didn't make the assault.

I got on the U.S.N.S. General Pope in Puget Sound, Washington to Vietnam in 1966 and ran into him on board 4 days into the trip. I was happy to run into someone I knew and we were good friends. I asked him why he wasn't retired. He told me he had six months to go so he volunteered. He didn't have to be there. I also volunteered and he knew that I didn't have to be there either, but I was 25 years old, hadn't been in combat and was gung ho. I wasn't going to lose my chance to fight for my Country but it was different for my friend. He was married with children and already had 22 years in.

During WWII in 1944 he was awarded the C.I.B. (Combat Infantryman Badge). That's what an infantryman earns for being in combat and under fire for 30 days or more. The badge bears a rifle with a wreath around it. He was also in the Korean War where he earned a second C.I.B., which added a silver star to the top of the rifle and wreath. In Vietnam he earned a third C.I.B. with two silver stars.

We got to Vietnam and he had me transferred to his platoon. He told the 1st SGT we had a history together and he wanted me to watch his back and vice versa. He was a man's man. He treated me like a son and I was proud to have him for a friend and mentor. We had a lot of laughs together and we always hugged each other along with a handshake. I used to joke with him saying that some day I would have all those ribbons that he had. I needed three wars! I loved him. Well, he had less than 30 days to go before he went back to the States to retire.

. . .

I keep yelling out, "Why! You didn't have to come here. Why, Pops, why." I can't explain how my heart feels. It's being wrenched and squeezed. It seems like everyone I have ever loved dies. I feel guilty. I should have pushed him in ahead of me. I didn't have his back, that was part of the bargain. If only I had gotten him in the hole a split second earlier.

I beg him for forgiveness. I let him down. I tell him I'm sorry over and over. I'm confused and crying. At the same time I'm mad at him for even being here. I don't understand, he had less than 30 days to go. This great man, it can't be true, not him.

I grabbed my rifle. I'm so angry I'm like a wild man. I want to kill each and every North Vietnamese. I hate them and want them all to pay. I have no compassion for any of them, I want them all dead.

Nurse Dorothy

I woke up again soaking wet. My heart trembling, I was a nervous wreck. I laid in bed crying. It seemed so real again. I wiped away the tears, I didn't want anyone to see me like that. I couldn't get it out of my mind. I prayed for my friend.

The nurse heard me yelling from down the hall and came into my room. She asked if I was in pain, I told her I was okay. She saw that I was soaking wet and checked me for fever. My temperature was normal. She said she was going to change the bed sheets and left to get a nurse to help her. She came back a few minutes later with another nurse and they changed the bedding. When they finished the other nurse stayed behind.

She told me her name was Dorothy and asked if we could talk. I said sure. She went on to tell me that a friend of hers was working in intensive care when I was there and told her that I would often wake up screaming, wet with sweat, sometimes crying and upset. Dorothy was concerned and asked if I was having nightmares about the accident, if

I was upset because I was told I wouldn't walk or if I had some other trauma in my life. She said if it was too personal I didn't have to answer her. I told her that I would like someone to talk to but I was ashamed I might cry. She assured me I didn't have to feel ashamed then asked me if I had ever been in military service. I said yes and wondered why she asked.

She confided to me that her husband had died a year and a half before. He was a Marine and had fought in the Battle of Tarawa during World War II. The battlefield memories had been traumatic causing him to have flashbacks. He often woke up screaming. He would cry and she would hold him and talk to him until he went back to sleep. She felt I had the same symptoms she had seen in her husband. I told her I had been in combat in Vietnam and that was all that needed to be said. She hugged me and we both cried.

I looked forward to seeing Dorothy. She worked the 2nd shift and on her days off I missed her. She was comforting, like my mother, and she understood. There's no one you can talk to about being in the war because no one understands except those that have been there. Dorothy understood. She had gone through the trauma with her husband and she knew.

We talked a lot and I believe our talks helped her mourn her husband as well. I guess we both needed help. She helped me with hugs and understanding. She would come in when she was on duty to wipe my forehead with a washcloth when I had nightmares and always spent time with me before she went home. She prayed with me and hugged me and we cried together. I know her deceased husband was looking down from heaven and knew she was helping a former Marine. Our motto is "Always faithful." She helped my spirits tremendously. I will always have a great big love in my heart for her.

Dorothy had a conversation with my doctor. I don't know all that she said but I understand she told him she thought he was leaving me without any hope. Because of the nightmares reliving the war I already had my plate full and I needed to feel I could overcome. She told him I had been through hell in the war and that when a person like me has all that happen, you have to encourage them. I needed to be in the same survival mode that got me through the war. I needed hope to help me strive to walk again one goal at a time otherwise there would be a risk of deep depression.

What a nurse. She was great, she gave me the gumption to prove to the doctors, and to myself, that I would never give up. Through that unselfish nurse I continued to work hard and dream about the day I'd win.

Flashback Five

I'm on Listening Post (LP) #4 outside the perimeter. It's night and I'm looking and listening for Charlie probing the perimeter. Two of us are in a hole with M-16's, four grenades and a "prick-6" radio. LP is rotated so that we each get the duty every 10 or 12 days. No one wants LP duty because if you catch Charlie probing and he attacks you can get caught in the cross fire. Charlie is firing at your buddies and your buddies in the perimeter are firing back. You get caught in the middle and you're a dead man. It's terrible because you're always worrying.

It's the monsoon season. I'm soaking wet, muddy and miserable. The jungle is pitch black, I can only see a few feet. I have to depend on my ears to listen for Charlie through all the rain, the animals making noises, and the movement of grass and trees. It is scary. It sounds like a Tarzan movie and my sense of hearing is magnified. Every little noise sounds really loud. It's nerve-wracking and I can hardly wait for daylight to join my buddies inside the perimeter knowing I had made it through the night safely and LP is behind me for another 10 or 12 days.

It's about midnight. I have a rookie with me who has only been in-country for two weeks. This is his first time on LP. We switch watch every two hours. I did my two hours and tell him he's on. I hand him the prick 6. I tell him to keep his eyes and ears open. Look all around our position, don't get lackadaisical or daydream. He says okay so I laid down in the hole. I can't sleep because I'm so scared. I try to rest my eyes and pray that the rookie doesn't go to sleep or we're both dead.

Several minutes into his watch Rookie says to me, "Ron I hear something. I think Charlie is probing the area."

I listen. I don't hear anything but the normal noises of the jungle so I say, "Come on man, I have to rest a little."

A few minutes later he says, "Ron, Charlie's probing. You've got to listen, we're going to die."

I tell him, "Look man, I'm scared too but you've got to stop this, you're making me a nervous wreck. Keep your cool."

He keeps telling me we're going to die.

I sit up to listen intently. I hear twigs breaking and I can hear movement. Now my heart starts to beat hard. I pick up the radio and call in, "Sir, LP #4 requesting permission to enter the perimeter, Sir."

He asks if we've made contact.

I say, "No, Sir."

"Have you seen Charlie?"

"No, Sir."

"You have to wait until you make contact."

"Yes, Sir."

Rookie says to me, "Let's go in anyway."

"Are you crazy?" I say. "First of all, without permission to go in our own men will shoot at us because they're going to think we're the enemy. Remember, they can't see us, they can only hear us. Second of all, we'll get court marshaled for not following orders.

He says, "I don't care if I get court marshaled. I'd rather be alive and court marshaled than dead."

I told him to quit panicking. He was getting me scared. I needed to think.

The noises got louder and seemed to be getting closer. I'd been in Vietnam for several months now and been through a lot but this rookie has got me scared and he's starting to make a lot of sense. I got back on the radio. I'm whispering because I don't want Charlie to hear me.

"Sir, LP #4 requesting permission to enter the perimeter, Sir. Charlie is all around us. We can't see him but there is noise all around us. They've got to be right on top of us, Sir."

He says, "OK."

I tell rookie, "Listen to me. When I tell you to take off for the perimeter I want you to run zig-zag. Don't fire your M-16 or they will see your muzzle flash. You have four grenades, two on each ammo pouch. Throw them over your shoulder and run like hell. You go this way, I'll go that way and don't throw the grenades in my direction.

We're in bamboo and we both take off running. I'm falling, throwing grenades and scared to death. I get back inside the perimeter and look like I've gone through a shredder.

The whole line opens up. Machine gun fire, mortars, and M-16's along with a battery of 105 Howitzers firing from inside the perimeter. A long time passes and we're not receiving return fire so we stop.

As soon as daylight breaks we go out to sweep the area. Expecting to find dead enemy we instead find a pack of chimpanzees. Dead. Shot up. Shrapnel all through them, with their tongues hanging out. I instantly became the laugh of our infantry company and man, I didn't live that down for months. They called me "Combat Kelly, The Great Monkey Killer."

. . .

Everyone I know has a funny story if they live long enough to tell it. I have several that are funny now but weren't so funny at the time.

I remember one day we were in our bunkers taking turns cleaning our weapons, checking out grenades, and making sure the holes on the pins weren't wearing out. If the pin falls out while you're on patrol you can blow off your arms and legs.

In the forward base camp area we have a few 55-gallon cans cut in half over a slit trench to use for an outhouse. This guy in another bunker is getting ready to clean his M-60 machine gun and he removes it from the tripod without removing the bandoleer of ammo from it. In other words, it's still loaded. He goes to set it down on the ground behind him. It's a little heavy and he drops it. Several rounds go off inside the perimeter.

There's another guy sitting on the 55-gallon drum relieving himself, daydreaming, when four or five rounds go right through the barrel. Luckily they didn't hit him but he got up and was trying to run. He trips and falls to the ground, his jungle fatigues are around his ankles. The poor guy gets up and he's got crap all over him. The guy who screwed up and fired the M-60 sees that this guy isn't hurt and starts laughing. That pissed the poor guy off. He's madder than a hornet and one hell of a fight breaks out. Needless to say, the guy who stupidly fired the M-60 didn't think it was so funny after he got the crapped knocked out of him.

My Mother the Saint

I woke up laughing even though I was in pain. It was short lived when I was again confronted with the reality of where I was and what I faced in front of me. But I was getting stronger and more determined mentally to fight back and win. I prayed to God several times a day to be at my side and help me. I knew He hadn't brought me back from the war to have me like this.

My mother was a small Italian lady with a big heart of gold. I can't ever remember her ever getting mad at me, she spoiled me rotten. She always hugged and kissed me which I loved until I was 15 or 16 years old and my friends were around. Then I felt embarrassed and I would tell her, "Mom, please, not when my buddies are around." When they weren't around I like to be loved and spoiled. She would laugh and tell me she understood. My mom was always so wonderful. She always knew what was best for me. God gave me the best mother in the world. I was a strong guy as a teenager but inside I was a momma's boy.

My mother never drove a car. She never yelled, never

drank or smoked. She worked hard, kept an immaculate house and made everything we ate from scratch. I always had breakfast, come home from school and have lunch and at dinner she always made a several course meal.

We didn't have a washing machine so she washed all of the laundry by hand. I had clean clothes every day. Because she didn't drive she walked to go grocery shopping and to do all her errands. After my father died she took a job working at Burger King washing dishes. She had a hard life.

When I was in Vietnam she sent me a package and a letter every day. There were times when the mail and packages got dropped to us from helicopters because they were getting shot at so cookies and cakes that took a week to get to me arrived in crumbs.

I loved Italian lunch meat and my mother would send boxes of Genoa salami, Italian cheeses and pepperoni. It could be 110° to 114° in the jungle so by the time it got there the stuff would be ruined. I'd tell her to send cans of fruit instead. Pineapple, peaches, and pears. She did and my buddies would come by and ask what mom had sent that day. It was great. If it wasn't for those packages all I would have was c-rations.

My mother was the talk of the infantry company one time when she sent herring. She knew I loved herring but man, when that package got there and I opened the box it stunk like hell. You could smell it for a mile. I wrote a letter to tell her I loved her but fish, meat and cheese could get me killed. She stuck with cans of fruit.

Now imagine this little Italian lady walked two or three miles to the post office every day to send a package to her son 10,000 miles away. That's my mom. I cried for her each day. What love she had for me. I was so fortunate.

I remember when I was 4 or 5 years old my mom said, "Ronnie, we're going to write your uncle a letter." My uncle Gootch was a tanker in Patton's Army during WWII.

She said, "We're going to walk to the dime store to take some photographs of you to send with our letter." I said, "OK." So we walked to the dime store and my mom took pictures of me in the photo booth and we brought them home.

I was looking at the pictures while she was finishing her letter and I started to think. Uncle Gootch is in the war and I'll bet he's going to have lunch soon because my mother told me after she finished the letter to my uncle we would have lunch. I reasoned that the war would stop and he would probably park his tank. He and his friends would have a picnic somewhere. I had heard there was a river in Germany so I figured they would be eating lunch on the banks and staring at the river. I saw no sense in waiting for my mother to finish her letter to send the pictures, I could get them there faster if I went into the bathroom and flushed them down the toilet. That way the pictures would be floating down the river in Germany, he would see them floating by and say to his friends, "Hey there's pictures of my nephew." He would grab them out of the water and it would make him happy. So, I flushed the pictures down the toilet.

A minute later my mother asked me for the pictures to put in with the letter. I told her she didn't need the pictures. All she had to do was mail the letter because he already had the pictures and he's happy. She asked me, "How could that be?" I told her I flushed them down the toilet. Uncle Gootch was having lunch so the war stopped for a while and he saw them floating on the river in Germany and he was showing them to his friends.

She looked at me and laughed. She said we would have to take more pictures and that she would explain everything after lunch.

My mother had the patience of a saint. I was a mischievous little boy. That's the word she always used. She never told me I was bad, she always said I was mischievous.

When I came home from Vietnam my mother and family met me at Detroit Metro Airport. I hugged my mother so much but I didn't want to cry. I saw my wife and little boys. When we got back to my mother's house she had a big yellow ribbon around the house and a big sign, "WELCOME HOME, RONNIE" and one big ribbon and bow around a big tree and I couldn't help but cry. I never thought I would make it back.

I love my family so much, especially my mother. There was a strong bond between us. My mother died a few years later. I miss her so much, and to this day I visit her at the cemetery 7 or 8 times a year and still cry over her.

12 Prayer

I woke up with a smile on my face. I'd been in the hospital three weeks now and I missed my life with my family. I missed my freedom and fresh air. I missed wrestling. My whole life had been completely turned around.

I started to worry about how I was going to pay my family's bills, how I would live like this, and how I would be able to be a good father to my boys.

When in need I always turn to my God and I needed Him now more than ever. I realized I wasn't going to be able do this by myself. I could work hard and do whatever was necessary within my humanity but I needed help from God. I knew He was not going to snap His fingers and everything would be OK. He could do that but He was going to want me to work hard and learn from this tragedy to become a better man. The greatest task of my life was ahead of me.

I started praying and asked if He saw it in His heart to help me. I asked Him to guide me and to show me what I needed to do. I was prepared to accept whatever He had planned for me. I prayed, God I know I don't deserve your help but if there's any way possible I would appreciate if I could get through this with victory.

All of a sudden I felt a power come over me. A wave of comfort like He was saying to me, don't worry son I will help you. I had tears running down my cheeks. I felt like a little boy who had turned to his dad for help and comfort and he said OK, but this was greater than that. This was my Heavenly Father. I had a sense of complete love come over me and this feeling that my family would be OK. As long as I had trust in Him, He would help me secure my goal.

I was determined now that I would win. I was preparing myself mentally. I was a near basket case but now I knew God would guide me on how and what to do physically. He would guide the doctors and make sure everything around me was in place.

I knew it would take a long time and a lot of hard work. I would come up against things that I couldn't even imagine yet and there would be times when I wanted to give up, but I wouldn't because I knew I had God's love and advice to show me the way.

Flashback Six

We're returning from patrol in the jungle and back inside the perimeter. It's the monsoons. We're soaked. It rains constantly. My buddies and I are getting set up for nightfall. It's a muddy mess. I'm filthy, muddy, and I've got jungle rot on my feet. In the monsoons you can't stay dry. Between sweat and the rain your socks rot, your feet rot, your underwear, everything. It's hot in the jungle but I'm cold from the rain. I have mosquito bites all over my face and look like a kid going through puberty. All I can think about is how miserable I am. There's no shower, no towel, no powder, no lotion. I brush my teeth with salt from c-rations. It's miserable leeches, bugs, mud, and rain.

We're in the bunker and it's getting dark. One of the guys notices a snake coming over the sand bags. It's a king cobra. He grabs his M-16 rifle butt, pushes on its neck and leans back. The cobra strikes at him coming about 6 inches from his chest. He's screaming for help. It's striking closer. One guy grabs a machete and cut the snake up into pieces.

What a relief. None of us had ever seen a cobra attack before and it scared us.

We man the bunker with our nerves on edge. Not only do we have to worry about Charlie but animals, snakes and rats as big as rabbits. Everything I never saw growing up in Detroit.

I'm scared. I'm miserable and can't wait to get home. Oh, how I appreciate the comforts of home. Hot shower, warm bed, mouthwash, no bugs. I dream of a cold glass of water, dry clothes, a nice meal. Wow. I pray God, if you get me out of here I promise I'll never complain and I'll be a good guy.

As I enjoy my daydream all hell breaks loose. Gun fire, mortars, machine gun fire. Charlie yelling "G.I., tonight you die!" They come in human wave attacks and the fight is on. I'm engaged in bloody battle and my mind is racing. I'm firing my M-60 machine gun and my whole life is flashing past my mind. Five minutes seems like eternity. I'm in a fight for my life and for my buddy's life. It's self preservation. Suddenly I'm in hell again. I'm sick to my stomach. The machine gun barrel is so hot it's glowing. I ask my buddy to give me the spare barrel.

He says, "What spare barrel?"

I'm firing and say, "The one you're carrying on your ruck-sac."

He says, "I lost it on patrol falling in the mud a while ago."

I tell him, "We're up the creek with no paddle. Throw the grenades. Throw them now. Charlie is all over us and is not going to quit coming."

We have 12 grenades. He grabs the grenades and

starts throwing them. He throws all 12 but nothing happens. Once in awhile you might have a dud, especially with the old pineapple grenades from WWII, but not all 12 of them. We keep firing. Charlie breaks off the engagement about 3 or 4 in the morning. Thank God.

One of our bunker mates has been shot in the stomach. He's hurting bad. He has his hands over his stomach, holding in his intestines and asking for his mother. I'm getting sick but I can't show it. I get the medic who takes over.

At first light we call for a dustoff medevac helicopter to get him out. They take him to the 82nd Evac Hospital in Qui Nhon. We were told that from there he was transferred to Japan where he was successfully operated on and went back to the States. I was happy and relieved to know he was OK.

After he's evacuated that morning we sweep the area. We're shocked to find that my buddy had thrown the grenades but was so excited and scared that he never pulled the pins. All the grenades are laying around on the ground. Man, no wonder we didn't stop that onslaught, he didn't pull the pins. We may as well been throwing rocks. Then we start to laugh. It wouldn't have been funny if we had gotten killed but that's how scared he was. Things like this happen a lot in combat. It's not like in the movies where everyone is John Wayne, calm, cool, and collected. If you're not scared you're crazy.

Hospital Visitors 14

Two guys came into my hospital room one day and one of them asked me, "Ron, can't you rip a telephone book in half?"

I said, "Yea, I can."

He looked at the other guy and said, "My buddy here works in x-ray. He doesn't believe it so I took the liberty to bring you this big Detroit directory. Will you rip it in half? I have 25 bucks on it."

I said, "OK."

His buddy spoke up and said, "I don't believe you. Let me check that phone book to see if it's been pre-cut."

After he inspected the phone book I sat in the wheelchair and ripped it in half.

His buddy jumped up and down yelling, "That's the greatest thing I've ever seen! It was worth the 25 bucks.

That was the beginning of a stream of visitors and fans coming to my room. During the next two weeks I must have ripped 20 telephone books. Nurses, patients, doctors and staff from other units and floors. People were sending me flowers, cards with notes and fan mail. People saying they were praying for me. I'm telling you it made me feel good.

I always loved fans and I never turned one away without speaking to them or signing autographs.

One of the doctors had taken his kids to see me wrestle at Joe Louis Arena and was a big fan. He asked me for an autograph to take to his kids.

They asked who else I had wrestled and I went on. Bruno Sammartino, Dick the Bruiser, George 'The Animal' Steel. Mighty Igor, Billy White Cloud, The Kalmakoff Brothers, Ricky Cortez, Lou Thesz, the six time NWA world Heavyweight Champ, Harley Race, Killer Tim Brooks, Bobo Brazil, Larry Zbyszko, Flying Fred Curry, Louie Kline, and Tex McKenzie.

The head doctor was impressed to know they had a celebrity. He heard that I wrestled but didn't know it was pro wrestling. He asked if I knew Andre the Giant. I told him I had wrestled him three times in three cities, Philadelphia, Atlanta and Toronto.

One doctor blurted out he had seen me wrestle The Shiek and that was a bloody match. He also saw me wrestle the sixth wonder of the world, Pampero Firpo, Gino Brito, Dominic Denucci and Dory Funk Jr. I couldn't believe it, these guys were fans. When my family came to visit they brought pictures of me wrestling some of those guys that I signed and gave out.

One doctor asked if I had ever wrestled Haystacks Calhoun. I said, "All 618 pounds of him!"

Soon all of the hospital phone books began disappearing. The head guy came to my room and told me I had to stop the requests because he had to order more books and though it was exciting it was getting too expensive. We had to get back to being a hospital room and not a carnival or gymnasium. He was a real good guy and would stop by each day to say hello.

Flashback Seven

I'm back in the jungle on patrol walking point man. We're right on the Cambodian border near the Special Forces camp at Plei Djerang. I spot NVA regulars at the same time they spot me and I warn my buddies to take cover. We take cover in a ravine. As I dive into the grass I get a punji stake stuck in my left leg. It hurts like crazy. We get into a firefight that breaks off in about 15 minutes. We have a couple of casualties besides myself.

A Punji stake is a bamboo stick sharpened to a point. They put human waste on the tip to cause severe infection or gangrene. I reach down, shut my eyes and pull the punji stake out of my leg. Blood starts pouring out. My leg is killing me. It's filthy and starting to swell. My buddy tries to clean off my leg. We're not that far from the forward base camp and it's a good thing. With the help of my buddies I get back inside the perimeter. The medic got a generator started up to boil water, ripped off a piece of shirt and put a compress on it. He tries to debris my wound the best he can so gangrene won't set in and then bandages it.

They finally got a dustoff chopper and take me to the 82nd Evac Hospital in Qui Nhon. They get me there and infection is setting in. They clean the wound and say I'm lucky because I could have lost a leg. They give me antibiotics. This will be my home for about two and a half weeks.

Every day they check my wound and change the dressing. I'm lonely but it's nice not to be out in the field. I'm lucky. Some of the guys here are in bad shape, missing legs or arms. One guy has a head wound that makes his head the size of a basketball. I help feed them. I feel bad for them and I'm thankful it isn't me.

• • •

It's around Thanksgiving 1966 when Martha Ray, the actress and Honorary Green Beret, walks into our quonset hut and starts talking with all the guys. I'm sitting on the side of my bunk. She came over and said hello and asked me what happened and how I was doing. She asked me where I was from in the States and how long I'd been in Vietnam. I told her where I was from, about my family and that I first joined the Marines when I was 17 years old in 1958. I then went into the U.S. Army the latter part of 1961 and then in 1965 volunteered to go to Vietnam. We talk for about 10 minutes then she says to me "Ron, what are you going to do next join the Navy and the Air Force?" I say, "You never know I might." We both laugh. She wished me well and continued to visit the other G.I.'s. She was so nice.

She is the only celebrity I ever met. I've never seen a Bob Hope Show or anyone else for that matter. I was always in the bush so her visit always sticks out in my mind and she impressed me.

After two weeks I got to leave the hospital for a couple of hours. I walked to a church in Qui Nhon run by French nuns. I go inside and there are people with leprosy laying on the floor in the aisle of the church. I have never seen anyone with leprosy and it makes me feel so sad. Their bodies are rotting away. I say a prayer.

Walking back to the hospital I see little children with bellies swollen from malnutrition, people relieving themselves in the streets, and people eating nuk mam sauce with literally thousands of flies on it. The worst ghetto in Detroit is like a high class neighborhood in comparison. I thank God for how lucky I am and feel homesick for my family.

Going Home

The doctors made their rounds and told me if everything went well I would be released to go home later in the week. I'd been in the hospital about one month. Under the circumstances I had met some wonderful people. My dear friend Dorothy, all the doctors, x-ray people, nurse aids, even people coming in to visit other patients.

A few days went by and I was released. I had many friends stop by. The doctors said they're going to miss me. I was given cards, good wishes and even a cake.

The director of the hospital came by to say he would miss me. He said it's going to go back to being a normal hospital again but for some crazy reason, he's going to miss the excitement that I brought even though the tragedy.

He told me I had brought sunlight and hope, the staff had a new energy and it was a pleasure to have me even if he had to invest in new telephone books. If anyone could overcome my situation he said it would be me. He leaned over, gave me a hug, and asked me to keep in touch. He gave me his card and said to call if I felt like it and let him know of my progress.

I got home and it was a great feeling. I was so happy to be with my family again. I gave thanks to God and prayed for Him to strengthen me. This was going to be the biggest fight of my life and I was preparing to win, no substitute for victory.

A few years before the accident I had converted my 24' x 24' garage into a gym. The walls were insulated and covered with paneling. It was heated and air conditioned. I acquired a lot of equipment over the years and had everything I needed. You name it, I had it piece by piece. Machines, mirrors, 10,000lbs of weight, solid dumbbells from 20lbs to 140lbs, olympic sets, and chinning bars.

I started by writing out a workout plan. I also wrote a letter to myself with all my goals, my expectations, my desires and dreams. There was a bulletin board in my gym and I pinned the letter to it. I read it each day as a reminder to myself and to get my mind fully focused on my fight to regain my legs. I was now ready to carry it out. It could take years.

My day was long and I was tired. Tomorrow I would begin. I went to sleep. My first night at home.

Flashback Eight

Fort Knox, Kentucky. We're on maneuvers and I'm assigned to 105 Howitzer Battalion which are M-52 self-propelled. I'm asked to be road guard. I go up ahead and get let off by a fork in the road. I have to make sure when the tanks came through they take the right fork. It's a hot day. I mean in the 90s I've got all my equipment on, helmet and rifle. Across the road from me is off the mil-

itary reservation. There is a farmhouse and a young lady hanging clothes on a clothesline. She notices me looking at her so I say hello. She says hello back. She is real pretty I guess about 23 or 24 years old. I'm 22.

She went back in the house. I'm standing in the road in the hot sun waiting for the tanks. I figure I'll be standing here for a while before the M-52's get here. There are three batteries coming, six to a battery. I'm in A battery but we also had B and C batteries so 18 tanks and 3 ammo sections with three five-ton trucks with ammo. A couple of two and a half ton trucks and several jeeps with the Battery Commander, Executive Officers, the Battalion Commander, a Bird Colonel, three First Sergeants, a Battalion Sergeant Major and all the support vehicles. This was a large convoy.

This pretty girl comes back out of the farmhouse with another load of laundry to hang up. She says hello again, I say hi back. She hangs up the rest of the clothes then walks over to me and asks why I'm standing on the dirt road. I explain to her about the fork in the road and how we are playing war games.

She asked if I would like to come inside to have some cold lemonade. I'll get court marshaled if I screw up and miss the tanks so I tell her that I can't leave my post and ask if she can bring the lemonade out here.

She said, "Don't worry you can sit on my couch, drink a lemonade and have a fan on. Relax, you'll be able to hear them coming. Tanks go by here a lot and you can hear them from a long way." I figured the same thing plus it's real hot and she is a perfect 10 so I say OK.

I walk across the road and go into her house, take off my web gear, lay down my rifle and sit down on the couch. She plugs a fan in next to me she gives me a glass of lemonade with ice. I drink it right down. She got me another glass of lemonade and an ottoman. I put my legs up and she sat down next to me. She is real nice. She says, "You're real sweet, I feel bad for you out there in the hot sun," then leans over and starts kissing me when I hear the rumbling of tanks outside.

I jump up, grab my rifle, helmet, and web gear. I say thanks and as I'm going out the door I see two M-52 tanks taking the wrong fork in the road. I yell at them but they can't hear me. I get there in time to catch the third tank and send them in the right direction.

A few vehicles later I see the First Sergeant, his driver and another guy in the back. I flag them down.

He asks, "What's up Zuke?"

I told him, "Top, two tanks came through and took the wrong fork."

He says, "What?"

I say, "Top, I know I'm in a world of hurt but can you catch them and I'll explain later."

They took off in the jeep, caught the two tanks, got them back and picked me back up. They renumbered the one and two tanks with the number five and six, no one ever knew the difference. They don't tell the CO.

· · ·

Top took me alone into the woods away from everyone and asked me what the hell happened.

He said, "You're a good soldier. I can't believe this happened."

I told him the story and he said, "Zuke, you remind me of myself. I've seen that girl before and I probably would have done the same thing. Women will get you in a lot of trouble. Have you learned your lesson?"

I said, "Top, it will never happen again."

He said, "I know. If it was any one of the other shitbirds in this outfit I'd worry but you're a squared away trooper and I hope you stay in and make a career for yourself."

I said, "Thank you but you're going to retire in a few years and I don't want you to get screwed up because of me."

He said, "Don't worry about me Zuke. I'll say you had to take a dump. You walked down a ways because you were posted by a farmhouse and besides they did push up the maneuvers by ten minutes. If anyone asks you tell them that story."

"Don't worry I'll tell them that story," I said.

Top took the weight of the world off my shoulders. I'd follow that man through hell and back. Now I'm an old goat and I laugh about that day at Fort Knox

• • •

Top was from New York. He had 24 years in the military at the time. He went into the Marines in WWII where he saw a lot of action on Guadalcanal. He got out in 1945 and took a job. Then in 1946 he went into the Army and was a paratrooper where he saw combat in the Korean War. Top had a Battlefield Commission during the Korean War and was highly decorated.

I learned a lot from Top. I learned how to lead men and how to earn respect from them. He was fair but firm and through his leadership I learned how to handle myself and my men at war and at peace. I also learned how and when to put a boot in their butts when they were shitbirds. He was like a father to me and I always did my best for him.

Top retired a Major ten months before I transferred. At his Retirement Ceremony he stood tall on the parade field. The Company Commander saluted him, The Battalion Executive Officer saluted him, the Battalion Commander and the Bird Colonel saluted him.

Then I heard Top, now a Major, said my name then, "Front and center."

I took a step forward, made a left face and marched. I made a right face, marched, then a left face in front of him and I saluted him. I didn't know why I was there. The hairs on the back of my neck stood up.

He said, "As the last official act of my 26 year career you are being promoted to Sergeant and you will be the new Chief of Section on the sixth gun."

Then he opened a box and pulled out his old Buck Sergeant stripes He handed them to me and said, "Wear them proudly Zuke, you've earned them."

Tears rolled down my cheeks as I said, "I'll try to be half the man you are Sir, and if I can do that I'll be successful. Thank you. I'll miss you Sir, and I'll never forget what you've done for me. I want you to enjoy your retirement. Major, You are always full of surprises. You never told me you were a Major, Sir. Give my best to your wife Sir, she is a wonderful lady."

I did an about face and marched back to my ranks. As I marched back I felt like I had met the President of the United States. I'm fortunate to be a friend of his and I'll always remember him. The greatest man I ever knew.

The Workout Begins

I woke up happy to be safe and at home. The dreams and flashbacks don't seem like dreams at all. They feel real like it's happening all over again. It's scary and nerve-wracking.

This was the first day of training to get myself in shape and to better my condition. I would start to force my legs to work and walk. I was in a wheelchair now and ready to put my plan to work. I gathered up my two sons and told them to take me out to the gym so we could get started. Ronnie was 13 years old and Tom was 11 years old. God blessed me. I had two good kids.

My boys started working out with me when they were 5 and 3 years old. I made them little 20 lb bars and 2 lb dumbbells and showed them how to use the machines with a few pounds on them. Growing up they had worked out with a lot of my wrestling buddies in my gym like Don Ross who won Mr. America and Mr. Universe Jimmy Hebert. They talked all the time about working out with Mr. Universe, Bill Pearl and Mr. Olympia, Franco Colombu. Believe me they already had plenty of experience. They were training with weights that 17 and 18 year olds train with and they knew more than most adults. They have been my training partners and were knowledgeable beyond their years.

We got started. They held me up so I could stand. I couldn't do any leg raises or calf raises but they held me up so I could stand. They sat me back down, I would rest for 30 seconds and they'd stand me up again. We repeated this six times. It may not sound like much but it was tough, especially for my right leg because of the severed nerve and resulting drop foot. In my mind I had to get the muscle built up to regain full range of motion and force my foot to be straight.

I could feel the pain. The boys would massage each calf and ankle then push me in the wheelchair to the chinning bar, stand me up and hold me there. I had to grab the chinning bar and try to do chin ups, three sets of six, then back in the chair. They would stand me up again and I would do three sets of six pulling myself up behind my head then sit me back in the wheelchair. Again, stand me up. I would hang from the chinning bar and do leg ups for my abdominal muscles.

Then they would push my chair to the quad pulleys and I worked my triceps, biceps and back. That would consist of three sets of six for all muscle groups. Then they would give me a barbell and I did overhead presses and behind the head presses. Then dumbbell presses for my shoulders and deltoids. Then I did dumbbell flys. I worked out for an hour and a half.

This routine continued for about six weeks. I gradually got stronger and could do three sets of ten with each exercise. At that point they strapped a weight belt on me and I did all my leg exercises with 50 extra pounds. This continued for about six months and I could walk with a walker. Each day I ate good food. I felt better about myself. I felt hope and I also knew there was light at the end of the tunnel. My Lord had given me signs that I was on the right track. I was psyched and wanted to work harder. I was tired and I fell back to sleep.

MONTAGNARDS REJOICE ON RETURNING TO THEIR VILLAGE. THE VC HELD THEM CAPTIVE THREE YEARS

Freed From 3-Year Bondage
By Operation Paul Revere

Story and Photos by
KIM KI SAM
S&S Staff Photographer

Infantrymen participating in Operation Paul Revere in the central highlands near Pleiku, Vietnam, have freed more than 400 Montagnard villagers held captive by the Viet Cong for the past three years.

Soldiers from the 4th Inf. Div. and 3d Brigade, 25th Inf. Div., on a search and destroy mission located a heavily fortified VC stronghold on Hill 1003, about 12 miles northwest of Pleiku.

Attacking in force, they routed the enemy and forced them to flee the area.

On entering the camp high atop the hill, the soldiers found more than 400 Montagnard men, women, and children who had been forced to labor for the VC.

Freed from their forced farming, labor and guide duties, the mountain people were able to return to their homes for the first time in three years.

On returning to their villages, the Montagnards were welcomed by their families. U.S. Army Civil Affairs teams. The teams provided badly needed medical care and distributed food and clothing.

Flashback Nine

I'm back in the jungle. We're on a search and destroy mission when we enter a camp and find the VC have enslaved a tribe of Montagnards.

They are mountain people of the Central Highlands. The whole family of five or six people live in a mud and grass hut built on stilts. They are naked except for a little rag they wear around their crotch, both men and women. They are good people and they love Americans.

They spend their entire life in the jungle no more than a mile in diameter from their village. They eat wild avocados, bananas, and corn. They carry crossbows that have carved out of mahogany for shooting wild game. They eat snakes and rats and they catch fish. They're resourceful and they make booze that will knock your socks off. They chew beetle nut which turns their teeth black and causes their lips to bleed. When I first saw them I thought they had black plastic teeth.

The Vietnamese and the Montagnards don't get along with each other. I don't know all the reasons why other than they have different cultures.

Anyway, we find this encampment of Montagnards who had been in captivity for over three years. Attacking in force we chase out the VC. The people were starving, the babies had big bellies from malnourishment. The Montagnards were so happy to be free and I feel proud that I was a part of helping them out of a situation of being in bondage and got medical help for them and especially the children.

Their ways remind me of the American Indians. They are proud, loyal people and they're great fighters. The men would hunt tigers with a machete and a crossbow. When they got one they would wear a tooth from the tiger like a necklace around their neck as a sign of bravery. I have blond hair and they all have black hair. They would rub my head and laugh because they love the color of my hair.

I feel terrible to this day that America left them behind to be tortured and slaughtered by the Viet Cong. They would tie up the village chief and decapitate or disembowel him in order to force the rest of the tribe in line. Our country should have protected them. They treated us well and I grew to love and respect their bravery.

20 Dealing with Pain

I had been trying to take less Demerol because I didn't want to get hooked on pain pills but the pain got bad at times, especially in my right leg where the nerve was severed. Out of nowhere I would get what felt like electric shocks in my leg. I was getting some type of medication to help the nerve grow back. They told me it only grows about an eighth inch per month and it had to grow back a few inches but I was determined to walk again. Slowly but surely I'd work my plan both physically and mentally.

I called my boys and we went into the gym for another grueling workout session. I was worn out but felt good enough about myself to fight through it and win. I refused to lose.

The boys massaged my legs. I added a hot sauna and whirlpool bath to my routine. The pain was terrible but I believed in my exercises and my whole routine. It was going to be a long and grueling process but I knew I was on the right track to recovery. I fed my spirit daydreaming about walking again, about being the heavyweight champion,

67

about being even better than I had been before. I focused on every desire convinced that it was important not to lose sight of my goal.

Each day was a painful struggle as I constantly tried to motivate myself. I had a vision to walk again that was my first goal, then to get my body in top shape, and to get back to the ring if God's willing and to win. I knew it was going to be not only the challenge of my life, it was going be against all odds. It would be a test of my being and I'd need a miracle from God. I had nothing to lose, everything to gain. I had given myself a chance again at life to get in a better situation to live in whatever was for my betterment and quality of life. I turned to the coin my mother gave to me when I went to war and read it again. "God grant me the serenity to accept the things I cannot change, courage to change the things I can and wisdom to know the difference."

I loved my mother and that coin was one the things I cherished most. Through that gift I always had comfort, love from my mother, and how well she taught me to love God and my Father in heaven to always turn to him and especially when in need for his comfort and to daily talk to him. I was exhausted. I got to bed and fell asleep.

Flashback Ten

I'm back in Vietnam. My infantry battalion is standing on an air mobile unit runway. Each chopper holds a squad. We get the order to mount up. It's noisy and loud and there is dust all over. We lift off, flying in formation, the sky is black with choppers. We're so scared. No one says a word but we all know that some of us will be dead in a matter of an hour or two. The enemy has been spotted and they're a large force. If we engage them a lot of men are going to be dead or wounded.

Every Friday, if they could, a Chinook would fly in bottles of Old Grand Dad. So when we load up we'd take a few heavy swigs to try and calm the fears. I'm not a drinker but I take a few swigs and believe me I'm so scared there's no way I could get drunk. I wonder if this is going to be my last day on earth. I look around at my friends and wonder if this will be the last time for them knowing that the same thing is going on in their mind.

While flying to our objective we sit on our helmets. Charlie shoots bullets that are ripping through the skin of the Huey gunship and we don't want to get shot in our private parts.

This particular day we have a new rookie in our squad. I take him under my wing. He is scared like all of us except this was his first time out, his first LZ, and his first fight. I hand him the bottle of Old Grand Dad and tell him to take a couple of swigs for his nerves. We're in close formation and can see guys in the other choppers doing the same. My 18 year old rookie is trying to chug the whole bottle. He's getting messed up.

We reached the LZ and it was hot. We're over 10 to 15 foot elephant grass taking on a lot of gun fire. The chopper pilot hovers as close to the ground as he can so he can get out fast and has a better chance of not getting shot down. He's dropping down and we're about 16 or 17 feet off the ground when this kid looks out, says to me, "Ron, let's get these mothers," and then jumps. I don't have a chance to tell him that we're too high. He jumped out and broke both of his legs. We hover and jump to load him up on a litter. We're taking on heavy fire the chopper takes off with the kid aboard.

We never saw that kid again. He probably went back to the States with two broken legs. He had only been in 'Nam about a week and I wonder what kind of war story he told his family and friends. All the guys had a big laugh over it. He had his 15 minutes of fame and we admired the kid. He chugged down Old Grand Dad, made one jump and his war was over.

A lot of things happen in war, tragedy, laughter, sadness, loneliness, loss of friends, fear. It made me grow up fast and it made me turn to God.

Getting Stronger

I t was another day to work out and I looked forward to it. After my shower the boys and I went into the gym. I kept my goals posted on a bulletin board in the gym along with pictures of myself when I was wrestling and in top shape. It psyched me up. I wanted to be like that and look like that again. I said a prayer and the workout began.

I had more strength now and was able to stand up and walk with braces on my legs. Believe me when you can't do anything with your legs and you begin to see improvement, no matter how small, it's encouraging. It brought tears to my eyes. I felt more than ever that not only would I walk again but that I'd regain all my body strength and health.

It was time to adjust my goals. I added machine leg extensions, seated toe raises, standing toe raises, hack squats with real light weight. I also tried squats with no weight with these exercises. I still needed the aid of my sons for balance. It had been almost one year. My arms, biceps, triceps, deltoids, and shoulders were getting their definition back. My upper body was looking good. My trapezes muscle, from chin ups, in front and back were looking good. My abs were coming back, my lower body still had to catch up. I was going to be symmetrical again.

I knew it could still take a couple more years. I had a lot of atrophy in my legs, especially in my calves where the severed nerve was growing back and it still had a ways to go. I still had electrical shocks that came out of nowhere and it drove me nuts. I never knew when it was going to happen and it hurt. I looked forward to the day when the nerve grew back together and I had no more pain.

I was satisfied so far with the gains I'd made but I wouldn't be completely satisfied until I was back to where I was before the accident. I knew nobody could take my dreams away from me and that I'd win no matter how hard or how long it took. My boys helped me back in the house to rest. This routine went on for months. I started daydreaming and fell asleep.

Flashback Eleven

I'm back in Vietnam, back in the jungle. We're engaged in a firefight with Charlie. I notice that my left eye feels scratchy and I'm having trouble seeing out of it. I'm rubbing tears away and having a hard time seeing the enemy. I'm thinking that it's a good thing it's my left eye because it's the one I close to aim. I look through my sight with my right eye.

The firefight ends and I go in to see the medic. I say, "Doc, I have something in my eye." He looks at my eye and tells me everything looks all right. I ask if he's sure because it feels funny. He tells me it's a little bloodshot, that's all.

A couple of days go by and now my right eye is feeling like the left. My eyesight in both eyes is blurry. I go to the medic again. "Doc, I'm having trouble with both eyes now and my left eye is swelling shut." He says maybe I got bit by a mosquito.

"Don't worry," he says, "don't worry."

"What are you talking about?" I say, "I've been in 'Nam longer than most in this company and I'm telling you I can't see to shoot, something's wrong."

Late that night Charlie hits with human wave attacks. I'm scared and I can't see. Under normal circumstances you're lucky if you can see 15 meters in the jungle when it's dark. I can't see 7 feet. I'm shooting blind.

I use my limit stakes which are metal ammo rods from the 105 Howitzer rounds. You put one on the left side of your M-60 machine gun and one on the right side so when the barrel traverses left or right, it stops at the stakes. That way you don't hit your buddy in the bunker to your left or right. Limit stakes are set up so that your fire crosses each other and the enemy doesn't have a seam to get through. So, I traverse left and right. I can't see squat and I'm so scared. I'm always scared but this is worse. I know I won't hit my buddies because of the limit stakes but I'm firing blind hitting North Vietnamese. The fight rages on, I pray.

The enemy disengaged before daylight and headed back to their sanctuary 2000 meters into Cambodia where they can't be pursued. I sigh with relief that I made it through the night. Others aren't so lucky.

My eyes are almost completely swollen shut. I have my buddy get the medic. I'm ticked off and not ready to lose my life over this rookie medic. I tell him if he doesn't send me on the dustoff chopper to the evac hospital I can't be blamed if I think he's Charlie.

He says, "I'll see what I can do." and takes off.

My buddy gets the Executive Officer(XO) and brings him to our bunker. The XO takes one look at me and says, "Zuke, what in the world happened to you?" I explain to him what's transpired and tell him that if I could see it would probably be safer for that medic to be in the North

Vietnamese staging area. The XO gets me on a chopper and has them take me to the 82nd Evac Hospital in Qui Nhon.

I later heard that the medic said he thought I was trying to get out of being in combat so the XO transferred him as a safeguard to himself and because he didn't want to be responsible for him when I got back.

. . .

I am as blind as a bat. I have patches on both eyes. I'm worried that I'm going to be blind for life. I go each day and get shots up through my nose and some kind of medicine in my eyes.

Every day my nurse, Patricia, led me by the hand to an outhouse they have set up. She put me inside and told me where to go, turned around and went outside to wait for me. After this she led me back to the hospital quonset hut and put me back on my bunk. I'd sit on the bunk talking with the other guys until later in the day when she brought me food and helped me eat. This was the routine. I can't do anything myself.

One day Patricia says, "Okay Ron, after breakfast I'm taking you to the doctor." I said, okay. So she comes and gets me. She grabbed my hand and leads me to the doctor. After that she leads me back and I ask her if she can take me to the latrine. She says okay and decides to take me through a shortcut between the quonset huts. There are 2 x 4's set up for a clothesline that the doctors and nurses use to hang their fatigues over to dry.

She leads me through and ducks under the 2 x 4's but doesn't tell me to duck. I guess she isn't thinking and takes it for granted I'll duck. The next thing I know I hit my fore-head on a 2 x 4 and I'm knocked down flat on my butt. I think someone has punched me in the head and I yell out.

She says, "Ron I'm so sorry. I wasn't thinking." I ask what happened and she tells me. I say I thought you suck-er punched me. I start to laugh and then she laughs. I say man, Patricia I didn't know what happened. Wow! You pack a mean punch. I said Rocky Marciano don't hit as hard as you do.

We laugh about it every day. All the nurses tease me and tell me if I don't behave they'll have Patricia whip me. I tell them not to worry... I'm afraid of her! They treat me well. Most of the nurses are 1st and 2nd Lieutenants. A couple of them are Captains and one is a Major.

I hold these doctors and nurses in the highest regard and appreciate the sacrifices they make. They put in long, hard hours under stressful conditions and they save many soldiers lives. They should be given more acknowledgement because they are real heroes.

I finally leave the 82nd Evac Hospital after 33 days. I get in a chopper and fly back to Pleiku. From Pleiku I join my unit in the Ia Drang Valley. When I get there, my right eye is still patched up and will be for another week. The CO says, "Zuke, you may as well go on R&R right now because you sure can't go on patrol with one eye patched. I'm sending you in-country to Vung Tau. You have been in 'Nam a long time, you deserve it. So go on and have a good time."

Rest & Recuperation 24

I flew back to Pleiku and wait half a day. Then I catch a C-130 and instead of going to Ton Son Nhut they say they're flying to Da Nang to drop off some prisoners. Da Nang is in the opposite direction up by the DMZ. I want to go to Vung Tau which is farther south past Saigon. So I decide okay, what's another half of day. I'll hang out with the Air Force. I get aboard. The C-130 is a cargo plane. The tail section opens up and it's loaded with everything you can think of plus a few Army MP's guarding some prisoners, some South Vietnamese, a few chickens, a pot belly pig all loaded up on jump seats.

We get to Da Nang, unload all the Vietnamese and prisoners and get ready to take off when we come under attack. Charlie fires mortar rounds and the runway gets all torn up. I'm in Da Nang for another day waiting for the runway to get fixed.

We finally get clearance to take off. The C-130 goes straight up like a rocket ship once it leaves the ground. We fly south but have to land at Nha Trang. We're here for half a day then we fly to Ton Son Nhut. At this point I've been gone two whole days and I'm still not to Vung Tau. I'm in the Ton Son Nhut Airport for twenty four hours waiting for a plane to Vung Tau. Picture a small pole barn about 40' x 60'. Most airports here are nothing more than landing strips. Ton Son Knut is about four times that size because it serves Saigon. I finally get a flight on a small Caribou to Vung Tau.

My R&R was suppose to be three days in-country. It's been three days getting here. I'm here now so I meet two Aussie soldiers and a Navy Chief Boatswain Mate. His nick-name is 'Boats.'

I don't usually drink but you can't be hanging around with these guys if you don't. The Aussies start drinking "33" Vietnamese beer. One bottle of this stuff will knock your socks off. They get four bottles, chug one down, talk a min-ute, then chug another. Not like Americans who generally take a swig, talk a little then take another swig. Boat's, is an animal, he drinks right along with them. Me, I try to but my head is smokin'. They keep it up and in twenty minutes it hasn't even effected them and I have five or six bottles sitting in front of me.

Now I'm drunk and the Aussies say, "Okay mate, let's go to the R&R center." We look for a rickshaw driver or a 3-wheel cab which is like a golf cart with a little truck bed. These Aussies are pretty big guys, about 6'2" maybe 215 pounds. Boats is about 6'5" and maybe 250 pounds. I'm 5'8" and 170 pounds. We can't find anything so Boats takes an Army Jeep. One Aussie sits with Boats in front, me and the other Aussie are in back.

Boats is racing through the streets of Vung Tau yelling for the Vietnamese to get out of his way. We have two bamboo poles. They're riding along on their bicycles and the other Aussie and myself are poking them with the bamboo poles and knocking them off of their bikes. They're rolling on the ground, cussing at us saying you #10, you #69 you #1000, you no f-ing good G.I. We keep laughing and popping them off of their bikes. I'm drunk. Remember I'm not a drinker.

After raising hell for a while Boats says he has no idea where we are so he ditches the Jeep and tells us we better catch a cab before we stretch our luck and the MP's catch us. So we do. He flags us down a little 4 passenger cab like I described. He asks the Vietnamese driver how much. The cabbie says 20P. Boats says, "Okay, take us to the R&R center."

We get in it's crowded. With all of our weight this thing is barely creeping along and the cabbie starts complaining. He says he wants more money so we give him another 20P. He's still complaining you got boo-coo money so Boats gets pissed off, flips over the cab. The cabbie is calling Boats names. He's probably a VC cause a lot of VC are in Vung Tau. So Boats and the Aussies say to him, set cong which means kill viet cong. The cabbie shut up. He was trying to rip us off.

We still haven't gotten to the R&R center so the Aussies flag us down four rickshaws and tell the drivers to race. Whoever wins gets a big tip.

In Vietnam they pay us in military scrip which looks like Monopoly money but has the same value as the American dollar plus when you get change back you get "P" Vietnamese Piastre. We don't get paid in green backs to prevent it from getting on the Black Market or in the hands of counterfeiters. I carry what I call my "AWOL bag." It's a small bag like you would use to carry your baseball glove and spikes in. My bag is stuffed with scrip and piastres. Maybe a total of $250.

My rickshaw wins, I give the bag to the rickshaw driver. Man, he is all over me, hugging and kissing, grabbing my ankles. I'm trying to tell him, okay, okay, leave me alone. He keeps saying, "G.I., you #1. I love you boo-coo, you #1." I've gone from a from #10 to a #1 in a matter of an hour. Who knows, maybe I made him a wealthy man.

We make it to the R&R center and it's nice. There's a big cement patio with umbrella tables and a brook of water. One arm bandits you know slot machines. Guys drinking Saigon Tea, whiskey, '33' beer, and Tiger beer. Maybe 85 to 100 guys in the place all Navy, Air Force, Marines, Army, Coast Guard, Aussies, and Canadians. Me, Boats, and the Aussies are sitting there drinking. I don't know how, I'm still feeling high.

A group of Vietnamese girls are up on stage singing like the Beatles. They sing real good we're enjoying them. The girls take a break and an Army Master Sergeant(M/SGT) in the crowd decides he's going to get on stage, grab the microphone and tell jokes. They aren't good. The girls came back and they want to sing another set but the M/SGT won't give up the mic. The crowd is getting pissed off and yelling for him to give the mic back so the girls could sing. The M/SGT says, "Wait! I've got one more." The Aussies love to drink and fight are getting pissed off. Boats yells at the M/SGT to put down the mic and let the girls sing or he'll kick his butt. The M/SGT's buddies start yelling at Boats and the Aussies. That's all it takes. I'm with them, I'm drunk, and I am in.

Boats gets up, grabs the M/SGT by the butt and the nap of his neck and throws him in the water, microphone and all. The M/SGT's buddies jump in on different sides grabbing umbrellas out of tables and swinging them, punching, kicking. The biggest gang fight I've been in. It's a mad house. The M/SGT is tied up in the microphone wire and gargling water.

Somebody called the MP's and two truck loads of them along with a Bird Colonel show up and lock our heels. We're all standing at attention getting screamed at. We tell the Colonel that we've been in the bush for months, we're sorry and we won't do it again. Like me, Boats, and the Aussies it's only the first day of R&R for most of the guys there. It doesn't matter. The Colonel says he doesn't care, called for more trucks and loaded everyone up. They took us to the airport and stood there until we all got kicked out of Vung Tau. Man, I can't believe it. I only got half a day of R&R in Vung Tau. I never saw Boats or the Aussies again.

Flying back took another day or so after making all the stops. I finally got back and showed up in the jungle in cotton khaki pants holding my rifle, my helmet on my head, thongs on my feet, and my boots strung around my shoulders. The CO looks at me and says, "What the hell happened to you? You must have enjoyed your three days in Vung Tau."

I say, "Sir, I was only there a half of a day."

I explained what happened and he laughed. The old man says, "There's always excitement in your life."

. . .

The CO was killed about 10 days later from an RPG (Rocket Propelled Grenade) He was a man's man. I was with him when he got hit by a piece of shrapnel. It hit him in the chest. I looked and smoke is coming out of his chest. He fell. That was it. I cried.

I knew him when we were on the U.S.N.S. General Pope. He was a First Lieutenant and then made Captain. He had been a Commanding Officer about eight weeks.

We both loved baseball and would brag about our favorite team. I loved Al Kaline and the Detroit Tigers and he loved Mickey Mantle and the New York Yankees. We both agreed that they were great ball players but we would always argue about the teams and the players.

He had been a pitcher in high school and college baseball and I was a switch hitter. We would argue. He said he could strike me out and I wouldn't touch him. I'd say I could take him deep right handed or left handed. Then I would grab a tree branch, he would roll up a pair of socks and we would screw around. I still see that over and over for all these years.

I cried I was sick. My heart broken again. I couldn't believe it. I keep losing my buddies. I tried to wake him up. It happened so fast.

I wanted him back so I could tell him that he could strike me out, I couldn't touch his curve. I wanted to tell him I loved him, but reality set in, we would never talk again. I'll never forget the Captain.

25

My Friends

I want the American people to know about my friends and to understand that they have freedom because so many brave young men and women sacrifice their futures. From the War of Independents to this day they give their all for the freedom of America. Think of these men and women in your daily prayers. Thank them and thank God that you live in America. I do and I'm grateful.

We are fortunate to live in this great Country. Far too many people don't realize how much freedom they have and they take it for granted. Freedom is not free. The price of freedom is paid for in the loss of arms and legs, in never ending nightmares, in anguish, pain and tears. The price of freedom is paid for in brutal death and horrors that never leave the memory.

The men and women of the Armed Forces leave their families for months and years at a time. They miss their sons and daughters, their mothers and fathers, their wives and husbands. Life will never be the same and even if they are a survivor like me, the mind and heart has lost all innocence, never to be recaptured again.

To this day when I listen to the Star-Spangled Banner the hairs stand up on the back of my neck and I'm caught up in the song Francis Scott Keys wrote so many years ago. I understand his thoughts and I can feel these brave men and women, the hell they went through and what they gave for our freedom.

I am so proud to be an American. When I look at Old Glory flying I see the blue as the many oceans we've crossed. I see the red as all the blood that was, and is, shed. I see the white stars as the souls of all these unselfish men and women, so pure and innocent, resting in Gods heaven, shining down on us brightly. When the flag ferrules in the wind I feel the last breath that many of these men and women gave for you and me. The tears well up in my eyes because some of these souls were my buddies and my friends.

One Year Later

One year later I was walking with the support of a cane and braces on my legs. My upper body looked good. From the waist up I looked like Mr. Universe. I'd been working my legs too but lightly because they couldn't take the grueling workouts. I worked hard. I did toe raises until I had tears in my eyes. The toe raises were for my calves but I was also trying to get the full range of motion back in my right foot. I did leg extensions, front and back and squats with light weight. My goal was to get my leg strength back and try to be symmetrical. I knew I still had a long way to go. I set my sights on my goals and was determined to adapt and overcome. I wanted it so bad, I could taste it.

At this point my money was gone. I had two sons to raise, bills to pay, a mortgage, and no insurance. I needed to do something to fulfill my financial obligations and feed my sons. I made a little money before the accident. Between wrestling, working concrete, landscaping, and driving a cab I had saved enough money to sustain my family for one year which included paying the medical bills. Now I had gone through it all and I was flat broke. The lawsuit from my accident would take four or five years. I was in a bind, which was on my mind along with everything else. I was worried about what was going to happen and wondering how I would get through this. It was time to formulate a plan.

Flashback Twelve

On patrol back in Vietnam. It's the monsoons and I'm miserable. I'm soaking wet and it's so muddy we have to hold each others' hand because our boots get stuck in the mud with each step. When you try to pull them out it's like suction cups.

I think about my wife and boys at home and what would happen if I die here. I'll never know if my boys will grow up to be good citizens or what they will look like. They're only 3 and 1 years old. Who will help my wife. I've brought so much fear to her life. She writes each day. She's worried sick about me. I don't have to be here, I volunteered. I was gung ho and didn't take her into consideration. She's a good woman and a good mother. I put her and my mother through hell because I wanted glory or what I perceived to be glory. I watched a lot of John Wayne movies. A movie lasts 1½ to 2 hours. The real thing is 24 hours a day, 7 days a week, 365 days a year and when you get shot at, it seems like eternity. It sure isn't like the movies, it's hell.

• • •

I'm walking point in Kon Tum Province. We come up to some Vietnamese carrying what looks like a couple baskets filled with wild bananas. They have a wood post slung over their shoulders with a basket at each end. There are several men and a couple of women.

As we pass they greet us, "Hi G.I. You number 1!" They smile and continue on. As soon as they pass our rear guard they reach into the baskets and pull out AK-47's and start shooting. They were VC. We return fire and kill all of them. They kill three of our men and wound four. One of the killed and two of the wounded are my friends.

I'm sick to my stomach and I blame myself. I should of checked their baskets. The rotten bastards. I should have put them down but now I failed my friends. I'm upset with myself. This will never happen again. My heart is broken and I don't ever want to make friends again. It's too hard to lose friends. Those rotten VC and North Vietnamese, they don't value life. I feel hatred. I wasn't brought up to feel hate but these people are cruel. They aren't satisfied with killing. They want to mutilate. My only comfort is that we got them all.

• • •

My brave friends gave their all for the red, white, and blue. They were the best of the best and will always be my heroes. They are twice a citizen. Not because of their birthright. White, Black, and Brown. Greek, Hispanic, Jewish, and Italian. They represented the United States of America they fought for her and when some of these protesters and goodie two shoes in Washington D.C. talked bull crap about American soldiers, I got teed off. They didn't know what they were saying. All they did was send Charlie a message and that message was, hold on. The people of the U.S.A. are going to complain and the Americans will leave. Hang in there and you will outlast the draft dodgers and politicians.

When people back home said the U.S. soldier wasn't moral I go nuts. How could they say that? They weren't there. Boy, I'd like some left wing radical college professor to say that to my face. All these people running to Canada, getting an education, or saying they're going to college and shouldn't be drafted It's easier to jump on the side of the radicals and say you agree with them rather than serve your Country. That way you could justify your actions and not have to admit to your family and friends that you're a coward.

I am a proud American and anyone who thinks the North Vietnamese won had better look at the statistics. We kicked Charlie's butt. Charlie knew he couldn't win on his own. We kicked his butt big time. He may have out numbered us but look at the losses he suffered, 1½ million. We lost 58,000. One American casualty is too many but his losses were 30 times ours and we fought with our hands tied behind our backs. If there had been politicians in Washington D.C. with any balls we could of kicked his butt in a year.

First we bomb. Then we stop for 3 months. In the beginning no one would bomb Hanoi or Haiphong Harbor. We couldn't go into Cambodia or the Laos staging areas to take out N.V.A. regulars. They could fire at us from there but we couldn't pursue. If I went in front of Congress I'd have plenty to say about their sanctuary and their rules of engagement. I believe that if you fight you fight to win. You don't let Charlie rest and you don't give him room to breathe. Charlie only understood power. You can't be a panty waist.

. . .

I come from a family of Italian immigrants who gave their all. They were U.S. Marines, U.S. Army and U.S. Navy. They were Tankers and Paratroopers. One of my great uncles fought with the Marines in The Battle of Belleau Wood where they got the nickname 'Devil Dogs' from the Germans in WWI.

Two uncles were in the U.S. Navy in WWII and an uncle served in the National Guard. During the Korean War one of my uncles was in the U.S. Air Force and another in the U.S. Army. My brother served in the U.S. Air Force then went on to retire from the U.S. Navy.

My uncles fought during WWII in the Battle of Normandy and Iwo Jima. My American born cousin named Dante was in the Marines and at 17 years old died on Iwo Jimo.

They fought in The Battle of the Bulge and they fought with the U.S. Army in the Battle of Monte Cassino and Anzio against their own people and Mussolini. They fought in the Korean War in the Battle of Incheon and the Battle of Chosin Reservoir with Chesty Puller, the most decorated man in the U.S.M.C. Some died hero's, some lived to become American citizens. Their greatest accomplishment was fighting for their adopted homeland, America the beautiful.

Among the first generation to be born in the U.S.A., I was raised to honor and to fight for the freedoms that my grandfather and my great uncles fought for in the three previous wars. I was taught to be grateful for America and to shed my blood to bring honor to her and my U.S. citizenship.

When I was a boy they would argue about whether I would join the U.S.M.C., the Army or Navy when I got to be a big boy and they argued about which one of them would win out. I couldn't let any of them down so I joined the Marines, the Army, and the Navy.

My Buddy The Gambler

I was worried about my finances and wondering what to do when I started thinking about my best friend Richie. When we were 13 years old Richie was always gambling and shooting pool. He was a chubby kid that looked a lot like Jackie Gleason and could shoot pool like him, too.

He had his own pool stick and he would hustle at the local pool halls. When he won he'd have me hold his money and tell me that no matter what if he started to lose don't let him have any of the winnings. No matter how much he asked. Then when he started to lose he'd tell me to give him his money and I would say no. He would get mad and start yelling. I'd yell back. Back and forth we went until I would finally give in and say, "here, take your money" and give it to him. He would go on to lose it, then get mad and remind me that he had told me not to give the money back, no matter what. It didn't matter how much he would complain, this happened all the time. Same thing with gambling, poker, craps, it didn't matter.

We were in the 7th or 8th grade and he would be in games with guys anywhere from 18 to 35 years old. He won a lot of money and when he won big he would show up at my house in a cab and pick me up for school (I lived a block away from school). Richie would tip the cabbie and tell him to be back at the school to pick us up at 3:00 and he would give him another tip. This was in the early 50s. The cab fare might have been forty cents but Richie would give the cabbie 4 or 5 bucks in the morning and the same at night. Richie was a character.

One Sunday Richie said to me, "Ron, there's an empty store across from the church and it's been for rent for several months." I asked him what he intended to do. He said he intended to rent it. He had been inside the building before and knew there was a basement in it. We could run a game in the basement. We were 14 years old then. I said okay but told him that nobody was going to rent a building to a couple of 14 year olds.

My brother had a friend who was 21 years old that said our plan sounded good. He was willing to work with us and became our front man. He went to the building owner and offered to rent the building on a month to month basis. The owner was agreeable because renting by the month was better than nothing. Then he wanted to know what kind of business. We had our front man tell him he was going to open a fruit market. The owner went for it.

Richie's brother was 18 years old and had a car so we rented a trailer, hooked it up to his brother's car and went to Eastern Market in Detroit. We bought bushels of apples, pears, oranges, peaches, cherries, grapes, and melons. We went back to the building and set the fruit up in the display cases that were in the front windows. One of the guy's grandfather had a poultry shop years before and we got his scale. We had a bunch of paper bags on a table with a scale and we contacted Coca-Cola for a sign. The sign said 'Richie's Fruit Market.' We had a cigar box with change and that was it. Down in the basement we set up five card tables that we borrowed. Richie's dad had a jukebox route and he lifted one for us so we had music. We opened up on Saturday night and everything went well.

After 6 o'clock Mass one Sunday morning we were in the basement when we heard footsteps upstairs. I went up and the place was packed. People had gotten out of church and everybody wanted fruit. I mean it was packed! I was going nuts. I didn't even use the scale. I packed bags full and asked for 50 cents. The place was a success.

So we made money from the games and the fruit. I worked myself to death going to the Farmers Market. I was pushing so much fruit. All the farmers and I got to know each other on a first name basis. I had farmers asking if I would push their cucumbers, lettuce, whatever. After a while the farmers started delivering right to the building. Business was good for everyone and in a short time we had a major market. The supermarkets couldn't match our prices.

I ran the market, Richie ran the games. It lasted a few months and one Sunday morning the cops found out and busted us. I wasn't there at the time but everyone got hauled in and had to pay a $25.00 fine, except for Richie. He went to juvenile for one night. The cops couldn't believe a 14 year old was the ring leader. The people in the neighborhood were upset that they had to go back to the supermarkets and pay higher prices and the farmers were upset because we pushed their fruit and the produce. Unbelievable, but true.

. . .

The second time I joined the Army Richie had a wild idea that we would go to Vietnam. He had been in the Army once and was stationed in Alaska. He said, "Let's go whip Charlie together," so we went to a recruiter and joined. We told the recruiter that we go together and it has to be Vietnam otherwise no deal. We went for a physical and to get sworn in when Richie chickened out.

Three days later I was on The U.S.N.S. General Pope out of Fort Lewis going to Vietnam. Richie had ripped a $10 bill in half. He kept half and I kept half. When I got back we taped the bill together and had a scotch and a beer each. He kept saying that if I had been killed he would have blamed himself. He kept hugging me and was so happy to see me.

The Casino

As I was remembering all this I decided to call my buddy Richie. I told him I was messed up financially and that we should open a gambling casino. Of course he loved to gamble so he was in. We were going to need big money and a nice place where the traffic flow wouldn't alarm the cops.

I continued to work out with the weights and get stronger. I knew in one or two years with help from God I could overcome my physical problem.

A week or so after my conversation with Richie I saw a 12 story high rise for lease in Harrison Township, MI. It was a brand new building with elevators and nobody was in there. I showed it to him, he liked it. "Perfect, I said, we'll rent the 11th and 12th floors."

Richie put me in a wheel chair because with braces and a cane I wasn't able to walk far. He pushed me to the rental building. The rental agent was a blonde lady about 37 years old. We talked about prices and the cost of the penthouse.

She kept asking what happened to me so Richie told

her about the accident and asked if she ever watched wrestling. She said she was recently divorced and she and her husband were big fans. About once a month they went to Cobo Arena in Detroit or Windsor Arena in Canada. She loved wrestling and her ex husband had wanted so bad to be a wrestler but he was too small and skinny. They had seen Dick the Bruiser, Cowboy Bob Ellis, The Sheik, Bobo Brazil, Luis Martinez, The Banditos, and Andre the Giant. She told us there was one wrestler she had a crush on, Ronnie Martinelli, but she hadn't seen him. She heard he and Johney Valentine both had serious accidents. Johney Valentine was paralyzed and some people said Ron Martinelli was seriously injured but didn't know how bad.

Richie was surprised that she was a fan and he told her The Banditos, Luis Martinez and Ron Martinelli were from Clinton Township, Michigan and he was close friends with them. She got all excited and asked Richie if he would introduce her to Ron Martinelli sometime. Richie says, "Yea I can." She thought he was pulling her leg. He told her he wasn't pulling her leg and that he was close to him, in fact, if she wanted he would get her an autographed photo. And also The Banditos. Oh, would I be grateful, she said. He says, I can get you an autograph now and I'll have to bring pictures tomorrow. She looked at me and asked if he was lying. I said no, he's serious.

All the while we were there she kept eyeing me. You keep eyeing my friend. She blushes. She says, he's cute too. By the way you never told me what you do for a living. I told her that I used to be a wrestler and that I knew all the guys Richie was talking about. She noticed I had big arms and chest asked what name I wrestled under. I told her then that I was Ron Martinelli and I was also the Bandito with a sombrero and a handle bar mustache and my hair was dyed black. She was so excited and she asked if she could kiss me. I said, yes.

The next day Richie and I went back and gave her pictures of me with Luis Martinez, Andre the Giant, Dick the Brusier, The Shiek, Lou Theiz, Mighty Igor, Bobo Brazil, Killer Brooks, The Beast, George 'The Animal' Steel and Dominic Denucci. She asked me to sign the pictures said she would treasure them forever. She was so happy and it made me feel good. It had been a long time since I signed autographs.

She said Ron, do you want to rent an apartment or the Penthouse or what and it's driving me nuts since we talked you mentioned something about the whole 11th and 12th floors. What's that all about? I said, okay. I'll level with you, Richie told you I had an accident and I explained the whole situation. It's now been over one and a half, closer to two years.

I explained that all the money I had was gone. I also asked her if she could trust me and I'd explain more. I asked her to listen and I'd explain everything she needed to know and if she felt she could do that, fine. If not I would certainly understood. No hard feelings. No problem. I told her I thought she was a nice lady and that we could be friends. I had never taken anything from anybody in my life and I wouldn't start now. She said she was ready to listen so I told her my plan.

I wanted to provide a place outside of Vegas, with gambling and drinks. I knew it was against the law but we would do nothing to hurt anyone and no riff raff. I would not let anyone in that I didn't know or hadn't checked out. I stopped at that point and asked if she'd heard enough to give me a negative answer. She said no, she wanted to hear more. So I continued.

I would set the 12th floor up to be a casino. We would have craps in one apartment, cut an archway to the next apartment, have black jack in that one, cut an archway to the next apartment, baccarat in that one and so on and so forth. Poker $200 antis and up. Next room $10 to maximum $200 bets-roulette and on and on.

On the 11th floor we would install a combination lock on the door and have a guard to accept I.D. and check driver licenses. We'd keep a copy of everyone's number and picture and if they couldn't pass security they couldn't get in.

We would install security cameras in the lobby and pay for a guard who would have all the pictures and a list in a room right off the main lobby. Her office would be on the 2nd floor. The elevator would have an operator that was a guard. The apartment tenants, or anyone else, could only go to the 10th floor. The staircase would be blocked at the 10th floor with a guard posted. If any questions were asked we would say that construction was going on the 11th and 12th floors, for safety and security concerns, no one was allowed. That's all they needed to know.

We would put monitors in every room. Also, like Vegas, free drinks and snacks for those who were gambling.

If she wanted to she could also work after her day job. She could wear a cocktail dress and serve drinks and snacks. Whatever she got paid by the real estate per week, I would pay her six times more for the two days plus a bonus for renting the 11th and 12th floors to us.

Gambling would run Friday and Saturday nights from 9pm to 6am. We would have a girl for each room and a girl to make snacks.

I wanted her to rent out the apartments on floors 1 through 10 first. As many as she could to get her commission. Leave the 11th and 12th floors vacant. Once she filled all the apartments on floors 1 through 10 we would stop gambling and she could rent the remaining floors.

She liked the idea and thought it would be exciting. She said she would do it. I asked if she was sure, I wanted her to think about it for a few days, but she said no. I told her to remember that this was a plan. I still had to work out all the details and come up with the money to pay for the furniture and renovations. If we could pull it off I'd get back with her in a few days. Then reminded her the best laid plans could still go wrong. I didn't want her or us to go to jail for gambling. Richie and I left. Richie told me I was a good salesman. He said he believed I could talk Henry Ford into buying a Chevy.

We needed to find furniture and gaming tables. I had $3000 that I broke down into one hundred, twenty, ten and five dollar bills. I put a hundred dollar bill on each side so it looked like I had a huge wad of money in my pocket. That's was all the money I had in the world.

Richie pushed me in the wheelchair to a local furniture store. The store was located almost directly across from the county building and courthouse. I had bought furniture there a few years before and paid several thousand dollars in cash so it was a good place to start. The gentleman who owned the store was about 82 years old and he remembered me. He asked how I had been and wondered why I was in a wheelchair. I told him I had been in an accident and the wheelchair was only temporary. He asked if there was anything he could help me with and I told him yes, I needed a lot of furniture. He said he had a whole store, plus a full warehouse and if he didn't have what I needed, he could get it.

So, we walked around the store which had three floors. He told us not to worry because we could use the freight elevator for me and the wheelchair.

We had several apartments to fill so I started to pick out beautiful couches, recliners, a couple of bedroom sets, and bar stools. I still needed gaming tables, curtains, wine glasses, shot glasses, cocktail glasses, and linens. That's the stuff he didn't have. I told him there was a place in Colorado for gaming tables and the interior decorator who worked for him could pick up some of the stuff at other stores. She had picked up stuff for me before, a real nice lady in her early 40s with great taste.

The owner asked me if I was crazy. "You want me to buy stuff from other stores and pay for it then you're going to pay me?"

I said "Yes, I'm good for it."

He asked how much I was going to give him down and I said I'd give him $1,000 down and pay him off in 30 days.

He looked at me and said, "Are you nuts? You've picked out over $30,000 worth of furniture plus you want me to cover another several thousand more and you're only going to give me $1,000 down?"

I said, "Yes. Haven't I kept my word in the past?"

He said, "Yes, but you paid cash up front and it was only a couple thousand dollars.

I said, "Yes and that's why you should trust me now."

I reached in my pocket, pulled out the big wad of money and said, "See, I'm not broke. I have enough money here to pay for everything but I need this for working capitol. I'll pay you in full 30 days after delivery plus 12% interest.

He said, "I must be crazy but for some unknown reason I believe you and if my brother was still alive he would take me to the crazy house." They were partners. He said, "Ron, I don't want to know what you're up to but I'll do it."

Within 10 days he had gotten everything and it all delivered. I kept my word and in less than 30 days paid him off. I could of bought anything I wanted. My credit was good no matter how much the amount.

There was a time in my life that I hung out at a few clubs in Detroit. I drank ginger ale on the rocks but I hung out at these clubs because I liked the atmosphere. Some beautiful hookers hung out there and a few burlesque girls. They were my friends. I'd buy them drinks but never used their services.

I went back to the clubs and talked to four of the girls I knew. I told them when they got done hustling the clubs after 2am there they could hang out at mine and Richie's casino. They could be there looking good and if they scored that was fine. I wasn't being a pimp, if they made money it was theirs. I wanted them to hang out to keep the guys excited. Men love to have beautiful women around and it would keep them gambling and spending their money. I told the girls I'd provide them with a couple of plush, clean, safe apartments to take the guys to, just keep them gambling. They offered to give me a free-be every once in a while but I always said no. I told them were friends helping each other out, period.

The casino finally opened and we had some big shooters who spent a lot of money. Everyone was dressed to the 9's. Some of the guys who came to gamble were pillars of the community. Some brought their girlfriends and wives. It was a hit. It was clean and plush with no jerks. It was like going to Vegas and it was good for everyone. The girls loved it, the old man at the furniture store loved it, the real estate agent loved it. Everything went as planned.

We had been open about six months when the mob found out about it and decided they wanted a piece of the action. I told them I would close up and they could have the joint but I keep the furniture. The mob wanted me to stay and keep the casino open but I didn't want to get involved. Because I had at one time helped one of their boys out in a fight at a restaurant they liked me and let it go.

We closed down, restored the 12th floor to it's original state. The real estate agent got most of the furniture, my friend Richie kept the gambling tables and we made a lot of money. It served its purpose. The girls had made more money on Friday and Saturday at our place than at the clubs in Detroit. Everyone was grateful and so was I. That was that, no one got busted and no one got greedy.

. . .

Some people have said, "Ron you're a hypocrite because you got involved with illegal activity."

And I say, "Yes, that's true, but I never hurt anyone." It was wrong.

I ask my Father in heaven for His forgiveness and sincerely mean it and yes, I'm a sinner. That's why I turn to my Lord each day. Like Jesus said, a healthy man doesn't need a physician but a sick man does and I ask my Lord for help daily even though I don't deserve it. I turn to Him like a child turns to his dad. I believe in my Lord with all my heart and I ask forgiveness daily and if there is anyone out there that I ever offended or hurt in any way I ask for your forgiveness.

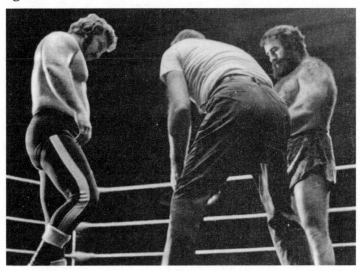

The Comeback

I continued to work out. I was getting stronger, now walking with one brace on my right leg. I kept working toward my goal and I was almost ready to get rid of my leg brace, a couple months away. My friends and my sons kept working out with me. I went to Miami Beach every six weeks for a year because I found that the salt water from the ocean helped my legs. I loved South Beach.

I got rid of my brace. I was in top physical shape. Even the doctors were surprised. I worked my legs hard now. Squats, hack squats, leg curls, leg raises. Running and jumping rope. My body had responded, I was hard as a rock. You could see the muscles were all cut up. I looked like I never had an accident. My arms and chest were ripped up. My abs were cut up. I looked like I was ready for a bodybuilding contest. I felt great. Now with the brace off I could start practicing wrestling.

Cemetery Salesman

While training for my comeback after we closed the gambling casino I came across a job opening in the want ads for a cemetery salesman and a grounds keeper so I applied for the grounds keeper job.

I showed up for the interview all dressed up. I had on a three-piece suit, a diamond stick pin with a two inch diamond, a diamond and gold watch, a gold bracelet with "Ronnie" spelled in diamonds and three diamond rings. The owner took one look at me and asked why I was applying for the grounds keeper job.

I told him that I was used to doing outside work. It had been a while but I could do cement work, landscaping, or whatever. I needed a job.

He said, "You're a well dressed guy. Certainly you must be successful. What kind of work have you been doing?"

So I told him all about myself the military and wrestling. I showed him some pictures I had brought of me in the ring wrestling various opponents. I told him about my accident and that I was getting well now, although I still walked with a limp. I said I would be making a major come back in the future. He said I spoke well and was an interesting person.

He and his three brothers had bought 170 acres and it was mainly cornfields, two barns, and a greenhouse. They were selling in-ground burial crypts. All they showed the customers was an artist rendering of what it would look like in the future.

You would also have a presentation kit and depending on location or how many crypts or what garden typically a pair of over and under in-ground crypts for let's say husband and wife. For property and vault and marker it sold for $2100. You would sell them preneed. That was so you wouldn't have to make a big decision on the saddest day of your life when you can't think straight and it's a terrible time to have to shop for your loved one and most likely get taken advantage of. With preneed you could make a good, sound, prudent decision in the comfort of your home when your not under pressure or distress. I mean it made sense.

He said I think you would be a good salesman I would like you for that position. So I said okay, I'd try it. I underwent training on all the paperwork, got a presentation book with the different renderings of the future gardens and went out.

The first week out I sold 8 in-ground burial crypts and made about $200.00 for each one. I was the only salesperson to do that. I went out on about two appointments a day and would sell about 7 or 8 out of 10.

So I figure if I make up a presentation for above ground crypts that cost $4000 to $5,000 I could make three times the commission. All of the other salesmen were afraid to ask for that much money.

My presentation took about 45 minutes. I always made an appointment when both husband and wife were at home. I'd shake hands, introduce myself and ask if we could sit down at a dining room or kitchen table. I started by finding out what their interests were and talk about whatever they liked. Then I would give my presentation. After the presentation I asked if it made sense to them to be able to make that decision in the comfort of their home rather than on the saddest day of their life and if I could make it affordable would they make that decision tonight.

I explained how they made a good decision because you would have to make this decision all of us had to and you couldn't get away from it. I would then make another 10 or 15 minutes of small talk and I would leave making a sale and also making new friends and about 6 or 7 hundred dollar commission.

I believe to this day that purchasing preneed is the right thing to do. Most of the people I met said it was something they had worried about because of experiences they had in their own families and how they felt relieved that God forbid if something happened to them it was taken care of and their loved ones wouldn't have to go through that on that terrible day.

I was successful. I sold mausoleum crypts and made good money, sometimes $3000 to $5,000 a week. I sold $120,000 to $150,000 a month in sales. I won watches and got bonuses in all the sales contests. I was the top mausoleum salesman. I won a Lincoln Mark V Bill Blass and I won a Cadillac Eldorado. Whichever car was the last one in my driveway was the one I drove that day.

The cemetery grew and the mausoleum buildings became a reality along with two veterans gardens that were nicer than Arlington National Cemetery. No more artist renderings, we had the pictures now. I sold overall $1-1/2 million in sales. I was proud of my accomplishments.

I became the Director of Mausoleum Sales and trained others how to sell mausoleums. A cemetery owner in Canada contacted me to come to Montreal to show his people how to sell mausoleums. He had a 40 acre cemetery and was running out of room for in-ground lots. I flew there and trained him and his sales people to sell mausoleums.

We became good friends and he didn't want me to leave. He offered me a home in Montreal with a car and more money than I was making. I turned him down and flew back to Michigan.

Hoodlums

One day I'm training in my gym and I hear a big bang. Some guys from a motorcycle gang had thrown a beer bottle and it hit my brand new car. I came out of the gym. I had tennis shoes and shorts on. I was lathered in sweat. I said, "Did you jerks throw that at my car?" Then I charged three of them. They took off running and I chased after them.

They were jumping over fences and I kept gaining on them. I was in great shape. Finally, they got tired, ran into a house and grabbed a man in his basement. His wife was in the shower. They barricaded themselves in the house.

Some neighbors had called the cops. About three cop cars arrived. One cop looks right at me, pulls his gun and says, "Man, you're too big to fight." I told him to put his gun away. The bad guys were in the house. I had chased them for throwing a beer bottle at my car. Some bystanders said, "Yea, that's right, they forced their way in this house." They were scared of this guy. They had machetes and knives. The cops got the idiots out of the house. They were worried I

113

was going to get at them first.

When the cops got back to my house, they went to the house next door and found a bank manager chained to a support column. The gang had been holding him hostage there for a couple of days. They were playing Russian Roulette and there were bullet holes all through the house. They had kidnapped the guy from a city about 30 miles away. He was so relieved that he was freed. Several members of the motorcycle club finally went to court and were sent to prison.

The cops became my friends and I ended up training them for many years. They would come by my gym after work with their bag of lifting clothes. They got a big thrill seeing me rip up telephone books. We used to meet at the bar and they would bring telephone books from home and make bets for a round of drinks.

I'll tell you one thing, I never again got a ticket. I was pulled over for speeding in an adjoining town and when the cop saw that it was me he let me go. "Oh, Ron. It's you! Slow down. By the way, could you autograph a picture for my kids?" The whole police department thought I was great and showed up at my wrestling matches. I had the support of the Navy, the cops, everyone. It was a great time in my life.

During this time I wrestled a lot of matches for benefits, raising money for one thing or the other. I also started promoting matches. We had good cards in different arenas. We had Bobo Brazil, Luis Martinez, Ricky Cortez, Bad News Jackson, Cowboy Rick Luka, and more. We were on our way back. It was a lot of fun and it made me feel great inside. We loved to hear the cheers of the crowds. Man, what a feeling! I will always acknowledge that if not for God I never would have made it and I give Him all the glory.

Mom and Dad

I was daydreaming about my life. When I was a little boy my mother taught me all about Jesus. I would complain to her about always getting hand-me-downs and she would sit me on the couch and tell me that I shouldn't complain. She told me a story about a little boy that complained because he didn't have shoes until he saw another little boy who didn't have feet.

You know, she first told me that when I was about 6 years old. I'm 70 years old now and I still remember that story. I try to live by the slogans she would tell me. To work hard if you want something and pray and if the Lord felt you should have it then He would provide in His time. Let Him know you love Him daily. Be kind to others and be forgiving. The latter is so hard sometimes. Talk to Him and always let Him be your best friend. And when you've been a bad boy, ask for His forgiveness and ask for His help. I wish I could have my mother back. I would have been a better son.

My father was a good man and hard-working. He never talked to me except to give me chores and believe me my brother and I had about 3 or 4 hours of chores daily. He was a disciplinarian. I would get angry but I wouldn't show it because I knew better. My father was as tough as nails. But you know my father helped me a lot. The main thing, work hard, don't complain, keep my mouth shut, and do what I'm told and if I didn't I would be punished.

When I went into the Marines back in the 50s the Drill Instructors were World War II and Korean Vets. They were tough but they were like boy scout leaders compared to my dad. He was tough and strong, and when other recruits complained, I'd tell them that my dad prepared me well.

M.C.R.D. Boot Camp
San Diego, CA

The first day I arrived at Marine Corp Recruit Depot (M.C.R.D.) in San Diego, California I had no idea what to expect. I went into the receiving barracks and was called a shitbird and told to forget everything I had ever learned. There were three Drill Instructors (DI). A senior DI who was a gunny, and two junior DI's. There were 76 of us. They told us they were now our mother and father. They gave us everything we would need in a bucket. It was called our "bucket issue." The bucket contained a razor, shaving cream, a toothbrush, soap, a towel, and extra razor blades.

With that the senior DI said, "You will be given one blanket, two sheets, a pillow, and a pillow case. You will grab a rack with a mattress. You will place your bucket under the rack. You have five minutes to shit, shower, and shave. Those of you who have never shaved, you will shave. Then you will make up your rack. You will then stand at attention in front of your rack. If you haven't completed this mission by the time I come down the line your ass belongs to me. Is that understood?"

We yelled out, "Yes, sir."

"I can't hear you shitbirds," he said. "Speak up like you have a pair."

We yelled louder, "Aye, aye, Sir"

Then he yelled, "Move out."

Everyone started running for the head and the showers. There were only four showers and we had five minutes. Guys were scrambling everywhere, tripping over each other with soap still all over them. Guys trying to shave, cuts all over their face. Probably 20% only shaved once every four months and maybe 40% shaved once a month and maybe 10% shaved once every couple weeks. A few, maybe 7 or 8 guys, shaved more than once a week.

I got back to my rack and made it like my mother would at home. I stood at attention. The DI started going down the line and he's yelling at everyone.

He got to me and said, "Well isn't this nice. Where did you learn to make a bed like that? That's nice."

I replied with a lot of pride, thinking that the DI liked me, "My mother taught me, Sir."

He grabbed the blanket, the sheets, the pillow, the mattress, everything and threw it all across the floor and said, "What are you a little girl, you pussy?"

I said, "No, Sir," and wondered what I had gotten myself into.

Then he did an about face and looked at the kid across from me and said, "Who in the hell ran you over with a truck and then beat your face with a baseball bat?"

This kid had never shaved before. His face was all cut

up and full of blood. He had even shaved his eyebrows off. There was blood all over. I couldn't help it and I burst out laughing.

The DI turned around to me and said, "You are a little girl, you pussy. You giggle like a little girl."

With that he rammed his swagger stick in my gut along with several other guys who had laughed and said, "You girls are going to scrub the brick floor downstairs."

He handed us toothbrushes and a bucket of soapy water. We scrubbed that brick floor on our hands and knees from 11pm until 4am.

I joined the Marines to learn how to shoot rifles and machine guns and to wear the uniform. I knew to keep my mouth shut at this point and go along with it. I wanted to be a Marine. I used to watch all the WWII movies. The Marines kicked butt and my chest would swell up. I might be a "shitbird" now but I knew this was part of the training and I was determined to finish boot camp and become a U.S. Marine.

I learned a lot in boot camp. I already had respect and discipline taught to me by my father. I learned to back up my fellow Marines no matter what. We were all one and in battle we win together or die together. We don't retreat. We fight to win and now I was part of a long tradition of U.S. Marines.

I would fight and act accordingly, I would never act or do anything to tarnish that honor, and I would always be faithful and true in the finest traditions of the U.S. Marine Corp. I was expected to live up to that standard and never give up no matter what the odds were. Like Teddy Roosevelt said, "Speak softly and carry a big stick." Never cause a problem but never back down from a damn fight, treat others the way you want to be treated and always call on God to be at your side.

I was in Platoon (PLT) 376 located by the 'Little Grinder' next to Convair Airport. We lived in quonset huts and always raking the sand around the hut so it was perfect. No footprints and no uneven rake lines, everything had to be uniform. We were at one end of the row and PLT 377 was at the other end. The head and the showers were at their end and consisted of two buildings that looked like wood garages. There were about 60 toilets lined up in rows. No stalls, only toilets. So when you had to do your business you had no privacy. If you were bashful you had a big problem. The showers were the same way.

Whenever we had to go to the head or shower the guys in the other platoon would tell us we couldn't pass and to go around the block. We would tell them to stick it and then have to fight sometimes 4 or 5 guys. When they had to do their laundry they had to pass by our quonset huts and we would tell them the same thing.

We were always taught that your buddies in your platoon come first. One day my buddy Bill, he and I joined together, was jumped by a few guys. I saw it. We won the fight. Bill, to this day, always mentions it.

We spent three weeks at Camp Matthews rifle range learning to shoot. Back then it was the M1 Garand the BAR 1911.45. We stayed in six man tents and you had to be asleep at 8pm. The DI would come in with a flash light to see if you were sleeping. Even if you weren't, you pretended. I remember one night the DI came in and he said, "Are you sleeping?" This one guy in my tent said, "Yes, Sir." The DI hit him over the head with the flashlight and said, "Now you are." After the DI left we all broke out laughing. This guy always managed to get in trouble. A real nice guy but he always seemed to say something or do something to piss off the DI.

Boot Camp was a challenge, some guys took four and five months to graduate, but when you go into combat everything comes together. All of your training comes to you and you react. You're fighting for self preservation, your buddies, and your Country. It's like everything fit together. There was no question that the training and discipline my Dad and the Marine Corp taught me and the blessing from God is what got me through.

There were four platoons in a cycle, 76 men in each platoon. We were constantly competing to graduate as the Honor Platoon in our cycle. The DI's wanted their platoon to be the honor platoon because it made them look good and the Battalion Commander looked favorably on them as well. It was a big deal and there was a lot of pride that you were the best.

Our platoon won the title of "Honor Platoon." We were so happy and full of pride. I received a few ribbons and medals in the war, but I'll always cherish the honor of being part of the best platoon in boot camp. We were sharp and that honor made us sharper. We even made up a song when we marched, I mean we were strutting our stuff. Everywhere we marched or ran the DI would sing out the words and all 76 guys would repeat. We sang on the run in the mountains of San Diego at M.C.R.D. Still today, over 53 years later, I remember that song and when I'm daydreaming, looking back at my life I sing it and it still makes the hairs on the back of my neck stand up. I still get emotionally involved and have tears run down my cheek. The song goes like this:

> By the light of the silvery moon,
> Marines will march in a single platoon.
> By the light of the moon we will march and
> march every night,
> And never back down from a damn fight.
> We're a fighting platoon by the light of the moon.
> We'll fight and fight each and every day and
> will never lose a damn fight.
> We're the Honor Platoon by the light of the moon.
> We will die and fight each and every night
> but will never lose a damn fight.
> We're an Honor Platoon.
> Our country calls, we're there to fight,
> We're a fighting platoon by the light of the moon.
> We are the best platoon 376,
> We're the Honor Platoon by the light of the moon.

I graduated boot camp at M.C.R.D. San Diego. I was gung ho, man. I made it and I was proud that I made it. I was in the fighting tradition of the U.S.M.C. and what a feeling that was. It was a big day in my life and I would do it all over again. I went on to serve in the U.S. Army and the U.S. Navy but I was always a United States Marine on the inside.

I was 17 years old so it was the first time I got liberty. I was young and so the only thing me and my buddies could do was go to a movie in San Diego. You know what we saw? The D.I. with Jack Webb. What a bunch of nuts we were to watch a marine corps boot camp movie the same day we graduated.

From Mailroom
to Supervisor in Six Weeks

I applied for a job at General Dynamics Land Systems Division. A few weeks later I received a call from their employment office. The office said they had received my application and that with all my experience I was over qualified for what was available. The only current opening was for mail delivery in their office building, which paid $7.00 an hour. The job was mine if I wanted it. I took the job and showed up to work the next day. I had to wear a white shirt and tie. I distributed the mail to all the different offices on several floors. I worked 40 hours and grossed $280.00 a week. My net pay was about $230.00.

I had been working for six weeks delivering mail when I was asked to deliver to the main manufacturing plant where they built tanks, M-60's and the M1A1 Abrams. There were picketers at the front of the plant, which was why they asked if I would make the delivery. I drove over in a van. The picketers stopped me and asked where I was going. I told them I had mail to deliver from the main office. Several picketers started calling me names. One guy with a ball bat told me he was going to personally kick my butt. I got out of the van, took off my shirt and told him if he felt froggy, leap. I was in great shape. He took one look at me and said, "Man, I'm sorry. I'd have to be crazy to mess with you." I told him that it was okay, no problem. I was delivering the mail, I understood. He should have understood that I was doing my job and he shouldn't threaten people with a bat.

I went into the plant and delivered mail to the manu-facturing manager and the plant manager. I asked the man-ufacturing manager if they needed a foreman. He wondered why I would ask and I told him that when I walked in I saw a bunch of workers sitting around and that it seemed there were a few things that could be improved on. I thought I could help him out. He said, "Oh, you do? And what makes you know so much about tanks? Aren't you a mail boy?"

I told him I was hired in six weeks ago and I got paid $7.00 an hour. I asked because I thought I could be of some help to him and myself. I had a lot of experience being a boss between hitches in the service. I had been machining foreman at Chrysler and also general foreman building the 318 engines. In the Army I was Chief of Section on M-52 self-propelled Howitzers. I had a lot of experience with people and a lot of knowledge. He asked me if I would go down to the line and show him what I would do differently because, in fact, Corporate was getting on his butt.

They were building a half a tank a day, 2½ to 3 tanks per week. I told him they should be able to get at least 1 to 1½ tanks a day, about 5 to 8 per week. Now he wanted to hear what I had to say although I knew it pissed him off because he was hearing it from a pee on mail boy. He said that he, the Plant Manager, and the Superintendents figured they were doing everything possible but they were still on the shit list with Corporate.

The overhead crane was setting the hull down on the line. They had eight people, four on each side of the hull. I told him there were too many people. Eight people and they were doing nothing but tripping over each other and screwing off. I told him he wasn't being cost effective, he only needed four people period. What he needed to do was put two people in an area to build road wheels then set them on a pallet. Get about two pallets ahead. One person with a hand truck moves a pallet of road wheels to each side of the hull. Have two people on one side, one putting on the road wheels and the other starting the lug bolts then use the power wrench to tighten them down. The other person goes to the other side and they do the same. The hull could then transfer to the next station.

At the same time one person could be hooking up the plenum, which would be complete by the time the hull hit the second station. If not, a repair person could finish and the plenum person would start again at station one. He would use four less people. Two people could finish any repairs right on the line or start wiring at station three and the other two could start putting on the tracks. By the time it got down a couple more stations you could marry the turret with the hull. There, you get at least one tank a day instead of half a tank, and without the overhead of removing the whole thing to a repair area. There would be less personnel with double the production.

I asked him how much he paid the foreman and told

him that I would work for $7.00 an hour for one month. If I got him set up, he would give me a raise to match the highest paid foreman and make up the difference in pay for the month that I got $7.00 an hour. If I didn't perform and get him at least one tank a day, he could fire me. All he would lose was the $7.00 an hour he paid me. He said, "It's a deal."

At the end of one month I had moved people around the way I envisioned, pissing off several of them, but the line was much more organized. By the start of the fourth week we were producing one and a half tanks a day. They gave me a pay raise. I was earning about seven times what I was getting delivering mail. About three months later, they started a 2nd shift and made me the shift boss. I got another raise and an afternoon shift premium on my check. I saved their butts and I could do no wrong although it was all common sense. I hired some new people and transferred others. We had a good team and I made big bucks.

One day the CEO from Corporate in Saint Louis came to the plant with a General from the Department of Defense in Washington, D.C. The General was the liaison. They were there to inspect the plant. Everything up and down the line had to be immaculate and no one was to talk with them except for the plant manager.

As they were walking the plant I looked at the General from about 40 feet away and saw that he was a Major General. I noticed the patch on his right shoulder. If you've been in combat in the Army you always wear the patch on your right shoulder. Your current Unit patch would be on your left shoulder. I looked closer and realized the General had been in my Unit in Vietnam. I didn't know what year so I paid closer attention. I could only see the side of his face but I thought he looked familiar.

Once he got closer I recognized him. He was my Battalion Commander. I held out my hand and said, "Congratulations Sir, you made Major General." He turned and looked at me, shook my hand, gave me a big hug and said, "Zuke!" I shed a tear and said, "Sir, I'm happy to see you and you look great with those two stars."

We talked for a few minutes. Everyone around us was stunned. He asked me what I was doing there and I told him how I started by delivering mail and had become a general foreman. He turned to the big shots and said, "I'd bet Zuke was a big reason for the turn around. You've got one hell of a good man here. You should promote him upstairs." Then he turned to me and said he would love to take me back to Washington, D.C. with him. I thanked him and told him the Navy had offered me a job teaching recruiters at their school in New Orleans and I was giving it some serious thought. He asked me to meet him at the end of the shift so we could talk over old times. He looked at the big shots and told them I had been "the best damn soldier in his command."

As soon as the CEO and the General left the building the plant manager wanted to know more about my job offer with the Navy. I told him I hadn't made up my mind but I'd let him know in a couple of weeks. He didn't want me to leave and offered to make me a superintendent. I told him it wasn't about the position or the money, it was about the challenge. I loved the military.

He bugged me and I left one month later. I had orders for New Orleans. I thanked everyone and moved along. Two years later I would retire from the Navy.

Winning the Championship

I started to wrestle again, small matches at first then back to Cobo Hall and Ohio, Cincinnati, Cleveland, Maple Leaf Gardens, Philadelphia, Pittsburgh, all over. I was back wrestling again. I won the Canadian Championship then the Continental Championship. I was wrestling all over the States. I worked out for a few more months and was ready to complete my goal of winning the championship. I won matches throughout the Midwest; Chicago, Toronto, Cleveland, Toledo, Cincinnati, Atlanta, and St. Louis.

On September 6, 1980 I got into the ring and won the Continental Wrestling Association Heavyweight Championship beating the Mad Iranian and accomplishing my goal. I wasn't supposed to walk, let alone wrestle, win, be a crowd pleaser and champion.

RON MARTINELLI

THE CHAMPION OF THE PEOPLE

by Brian Ashley II

It's a packed wrestling arena. Thousands of fans are in the stands. One wrestler is in the ring, pacing back and forth. Anticipation is high. Then, over the loudspeaker, the music from the hit movie "Rocky" blares. From the back of the arena comes running a man carrying an American flag, smiling and acknowledging the cascade of cheers. It's none other than the people's champion, Ron Martinelli.

The Ron Martinelli story is nothing short of amazing. It is hard to believe that this man was once told that he would never walk again, let alone wrestle! But, it's all true. (The complete story will be told in the forthcoming book, "Heaven, Iron And Me - The Ron Martinelli Story")

Briefly, some time ago, Ron Martinelli was wrestling from coast-to-coast nightly. His career was gaining momentum. He was beginning to decisively win every match. Then, a freak accident nearly destroyed him. He was pinned against a wall by an out-of-control truck. Rushed to the hospital, the stricken Martinelli was saved by a team of surgeons. But he was given the depressing news "You'll never walk again."

To an athelete, this is same as telling a painter he'd never have use of his hands again. Martinelli was absolutely stunned. At first, he took it badly. But as time went on, he became determined to defy the odds. He vowed to himself that he wouldn't give up. Through self-therapy, Martinelli regained control of his legs. Eventually, still against doctor's orders, he began working out with weights again. As months went by, he worked harder and harder at regaining top physical condition. And although he could now walk somewhat normally, it was absurd to think he'd ever again be in the ring.

But Ron Martinelli is not a quitter. His dream was to win the wrestling championship. And this dream - nearly destroyed - lingered in his mind while he was learning how to walk all over again., As time went on, he increased his physical activities....and the rest is history.

Today, you'd never know that Ron Martinelli was considered a near "basket case". Because he fulfilled his dream. He went on to return to the wrestling ring and to eventually win the Continental Wrestling Association Heavyweight Championship. And he's defended it nightly in towns all over the midwest. It's the same old scrappy style that Ron Martinelli displayed before the accident. Only now, his determination to win and stay winning is greater.

You see, Ron Martinelli has been through a lot to get to the top. And now, he's there. It took years of suffering and Martinelli isn't about to give it up to anybody.

Ron says, "Nobody has any idea of what I went through. While I was on my back in the hospital, guys like Blackjack Luka, The Mad Iranian and the rest, they were out wrestling every night, making names for themselves. They've got those extra years I was out. But I've got the determination and the spirit to never give in to anyone. After what I've been through, I'm not quittin' now!"

That's the spirit of Ron Martinelli, truly the hero to wrestling's fans. He wears the C.W.A. belt proudly...and deservedly so.

The U.S. Navy

I ran out of money again and joined the Navy Reserve. I made it through the physical and started with the Navy Seabees. After a few months I volunteered to go active. They made me a Recruiter. I helped kids until late at night so they could pass their test. I was supposed to put in 7 recruits, I put in 23. I had a way with kids and always told them the truth. I would not paint a rosy picture and I did everything I could to help them reach their goals.

I was the best Recruiter in the area, winning recruiter of the month by putting in 18 sailors. I won 12 gold wreath awards and accommodations from Cruit Corp out of Great Lakes, Illinois. The Navy sent me to school in Columbus, Ohio to become a Zone Supervisor. I was transferred to Washington, D.C. where I was in charge of recruiters in Washington, D.C., Virginia, and Maryland. I won more awards for best zone supervisor. My recruiters and I put the most recruits in the Navy.

I transferred back to Michigan and finished off as Navy Zone Supervisor covering all of Michigan.

While I was a recruiter the Navy ran an article on me in the *Smoke Signal* about winning the professional wrestling championship.

I had a well-rounded career in the Marines, Army, and Navy. I love America. I had many awards and decorations from each branch when I finally got out of the service.

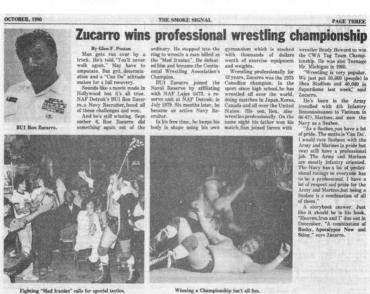

OCTOBER, 1980   THE SMOKE SIGNAL   PAGE THREE

Zucarro wins professional wrestling championship

By Glen F. Poston

Man gets run over by a truck. He's told, "You'll never walk again." May have to amputate. But grit, determination and a "Can Do" attitude makes for a full recovery.

Sounds like a movie made in Hollywood but it's all true. NAF Detroit's BU1 Ron Zucarro, a Navy Recruiter, faced all of these challenges and won. And he's still winning. September 6, Ron Zucarro did something again out of the ordinary. He stepped into the ring to wrestle a man billed as the "Mad Iranian". He defeated him and became the Continental Wrestling Association's Champion.

BU1 Zucarro joined the Naval Reserve by affiliating with NAF Lajes 0473, a reserve unit at NAF Detroit; in July 1979. Six months later, he became an active Navy Recruiter.

In his free time, he keeps his body in shape using his own gymnasium which is stocked with thousands of dollars worth of exercise equipment and weights.

Wrestling professionally for 12 years, Zucarro was the 1975 Canadian champion. In the sport since high school, he has wrestled all over the world, doing matches in Japan, Korea, Canada and all over the United States. His son, Ron, also wrestles professionally. On the same night his father won his match, Ron joined forces with wrestler Brady Howard to win the CWA Tag Team Championship. He was also Teenage Mr. Michigan in 1980.

"Wrestling is very popular. We just put 35,000 (people) in Shea Stadium and 40,000 in Superdome last week," said Zucarro.

"He's been in the Army (recalled with 4th Infantry Reconnoissance to Vietnam in 66-67), Marines, and now the Navy as a Seabee.

"As a Seabee, you have a lot of pride. The motto is 'Can Do'. I would rate Seabees with the Army and Marines in pride but (we) still have a professional job. The Army and Marines are mostly infantry oriented. The Navy has a lot of professional ratings so everyone has to be a professional. I have a lot of respect and pride for the Army and Marines, but being a Seabee is a combination of all of them."

A storybook answer. Just like it should be in his book, "Heaven, Iron and I" due out in December. "A combination of Rocky, Apocalypse Now and Sting," says Zucarro.

BU1 Ron Zucarro.

Fighting "Mad Iranian" calls for special tactics.

Winning a Championship isn't all fun.

Construction Company

I started Rinaldo's Construction Company with my two sons, Ron and Tom. My youngest son, Joey, and my grandsons passed out advertisement flyers. I worked out a lease with Caterpillar to buy some heavy equipment. I got two bulldozers, a loader, two small dump trucks, a Mack truck with a 30 yard dump, and a low boy trailer. We started by doing some jobs for the cost of materials and labor to prove ourselves in order to get larger jobs.

I had some construction background from the Navy Seabees and also from when I was a boy doing cement work with my Dad. Mostly I read books, asked questions and went out and sold myself, and my sons. I figured if anybody could do it, we would. I let everybody know we could handle anything. My dad used to tell me when I was a kid, "if you do something, do it well or don't do it at all." I demanded quality and everything we did had to be perfect. We did everything like we were doing it for our own home or project. Our prices weren't the lowest or the highest, but we sold our quality and always went the extra mile. We paid everyone who worked with us well. Both my sons and I studied for, passed and received our builder's licenses. In a matter of weeks we had a successful business.

We won a $150,000.00 job busting out and replacing the concrete walkways and curbs at a big mall. We also won a job for over half a million dollars placing underground sewers and parking lots for an industrial factory. We did a lot of excavating work on new houses. We built new houses, log homes, and decks. We finished basements, did landscaping and condominium grading. Anything people requested. We worked 16 to 18 hours a day, 7 days a week.

My belief is if you want something bad enough, go after it. Don't doubt yourself. Ask God for help. Be fair and honest. Work hard. Keep your sights on your goal and have the guts to go after it. Don't use the excuse that you've never done it before or that you don't have the equipment or the money. There are a million excuses. Go and make it happen. Don't let any obstacle get in your way. Be a high charger. Believe in yourself, pray to God and give Him all the glory. If you truly believe, you can move mountains!

A couple of years later my doctor discovered I had diabetes. I had to take pills and shots every day. Shortly after he sent me for a stress test because of the diabetes. I failed the test. The next day they did an EKG and I failed. I had quadruple bypass surgery. The construction company ended.

The Ballpark

After the bypass surgery I wasn't able to work construction so I bought a farm with over 100 acres. We had beef cattle, sheep, goats, turkeys, and chickens. I knew a little about vegetable gardens because my Dad always had a big garden and my brother and I turned it over by hand, picked weeds, and learned to rotate crops from year to year, but I didn't know anything about raising animals.

I joined the Marines when I was 17 and had only gone through the 10th grade. I earned a GED when I was in the Service. I was limited in my education, but I read everything I could about the things that interested me. I talked to people that knew and I asked questions. And like I've said before, I asked God every time for direction.

So, I learned about farming by reading, asking a lot of farmers a lot of questions and going to the Michigan State University Ag Expo. I loved the farm. It was a wonderful place to raise children and grandchildren.

As time went on and I became an old goat I decided that I needed a hobby. I love sports and my youngest son Joey and my grandsons loved to play baseball. I always had fun teaching them how to play, hit, pitch, and field. They started playing T-ball when they were 4 years old and went on to play little league.

There was nothing wrong with little league baseball, but I thought the competition was better in Fed baseball so I formed a team in a Fed baseball league. I told my boys that only the best played and they had to try out for the team, there would be no nepotism. I always told them to practice and that they would have more fun when they did well. I wanted to instill in them that no matter what they did, they should always strive to be the best at it.

We had kids from all over the Metro Detroit area that tried out for the team. My boys made the team. They didn't always start but they loved the game and eventually became real good ball players. They practiced everyday and in the winter they practiced indoors.

I formed two teams, a 9-10 year old team and 11-12 year old team. There were 15 kids on each team. Each kid got a Pittsburgh Pirates major league uniform and a sports bag. We had 16 dozen baseballs for games and 7 dozen for practice. Each team had two complete sets of catchers equipment. The kids had their own bats plus 8 additional bats per team.

Soon it became difficult to find a place with a baseball field that would let us play or that could accommodate our schedule. It became a problem. We needed a ballpark to play and practice. I had over 100 acres so I took about 7 acres and built a ballpark. I had bulldozers, loaders and tractors from the construction company.

I built the ballpark using the same dimensions as Tiger Stadium in Detroit, 375 in the power alleys. Bricked in dugouts and bullpens for each team with 40 foot foul posts in left and right field and a back stop 30 feet high and 72 feet across. The backstop had netting on top. I built a press box up above and behind the back stop with a P.A. system and had a 40 foot flag pole in center field. Beautiful grass, a 20 foot warning track, orange clay in the field and a pitchers mound. Everything major league. I painted the lines on the field.

The field itself was 3.5 acres inside and 3.5 acres outside. I put in grass on the perimeter of the park so the baseballs wouldn't get lost on home runs or fouls. I built a parking lot with curbs that held 150 cars and a 200 foot road. We had a 60' x 20' concession stand equipped with a stove, refrigerator, and freezer where we served cold pop, fresh pizza, ice cream, hot dogs, chips, candy, and popcorn. There were bleachers for 150 people with plenty of room for lawn chairs and umbrellas. Everything was free except for the food and drinks.

I announced each player on the sidelines and played the National Anthem before each game. We played music between innings and had announcers like in the major leagues. Between the season games, play-off games, tournaments and championships we played 40 to 45 games a season. I hired two umpires per game for $40.00 each. It was expensive but a lot of fun and a great experience for the kids.

Word of mouth started to spread while we were building the ballpark and I started to get calls from sports radio and talk shows all over the country. Local TV news and sports channels came out and did interviews.

One morning I was out feeding the cattle and said to my son, who in the heck is going to call next, 20/20? It wasn't a half hour later that my son came out of the barn and said, "Hey Dad! Tom Brokaw from NBC Nightly News in New York is on the phone and he wants to talk to you.

I said, "Cut it out and quit screwing around, I'm busy feeding the cattle."

He said, "Dad I mean it. Pick up the extension in the barn."

I said, "No, you're pissing me off. I would have to walk about 160 feet and the laugh is on me.

He insisted, "Dad honest, he's on the phone."

So I said, "Okay but if you're screwing around with me I'm going to kick your butt.

I walked into the barn and picked up the phone. The voice on the other end said, "Is this Ron?"

I said, "Yes, it is."

He said, "How are you? This is Tom Brokaw from NBC Nightly News in New York. We would like to send a camera crew out there to film the new ballpark you're building. Would that be okay?"

I said, yes.

The next morning the crew showed up at the farm and spent the day filming. The following friday night Tom Brokaw aired a 10 minute segment about the ballpark.

I began getting even more calls from TV and radio. It was a nice ballpark but I didn't see what the big deal was. I wanted the kids to have a place to practice and play baseball without a hassle.

ON THE PITCHER'S MOUND. Ronald Zuccarro (on crutches due to an ankle sprain) and son Tom look towards home plate of his ball field on Omo Road.

(Observer photos by John Jamieson)

Ray man builds his own field of dreams, but with playing time restriction

RONALD ZUCCARO

by JOHN JAMIESON
Observer Staff Writer

The crack of the bat hitting the ball and the cheers and cries of children enjoying America's pastime prompted one Ray Township man to create his own "Field of Dreams."

Ronald Zuccarro of 59699 Omo Road said he saw a lack of opportunities for area children to play baseball. So, he began to build his own baseball diamond approximately one year ago on his 102-acre farm to provide a place for federation baseball teams to play.

However, he ran into a snag a month ago when the Ray Township building inspector placed a stop work order on the diamond. According to township officials, such a facility requires large-scale recreation zoning.

The Ray Township Planning Commission granted the zoning Tuesday, Dec. 13, restricting use to daylight hours on Saturday and Sunday and one day during the week.

The commission meeting was packed by approximately

the team out of a childhood love for the game and worries that not enough children have the opportunity to play. Zuccarro turned to federation baseball for the solution. Federation baseball is composed of privately-assembled teams who compete with one another in a league.

The team Zuccarro is assembling will be made up of Ray Township youths and will be named the Ray Township Chiefs.

The Chiefs, composed of 11 to 12-year-olds, will play teams from places such as Flint, Rochester and Fraser.

"We are going to have one heck of a ball club," Zuccarro said, smiling.

Working with his son Tom, 29, he expects the diamond to be completed by April 1, in time for one month of training before the games are scheduled to begin May 1.

Meditation at Memorial

40

Nowadays I go to my son Joeys' barber shop and hang out with the guys. I meet a lot of old vets like myself. We tell war stories and reminisce.

I built a memorial outside the barber shop with a 30 foot flag pole flying Old Glory. There's a large circle of cement around the pole with a 24" diameter seal for each branch of service set into the cement. There are 12" x 18" American flags on each side of the sidewalk with vases of red, white, and blue carnations in between each flag on both sides. There is an intercom system and we have a CD and we play the National Anthem, God Bless America, Taps, and the Service Song for each branch of the Armed Services. The vets love it.

I wrote a poem called 'A Soldier's Lament' that I had laser engraved in granite and set in the cement. It says:

"With honor, courage, and valor my friends fought by my side in the jungles of Vietnam. Some lived, but many died. Rest in God's arms in heaven, my friends, for you have spent your time in hell. My war will never end until I see your faces again. -Ron Zuccaro."

I have a larger memorial at my home with seven flag poles in a half circle. A 5' x 8' American flag flys in the center on a 30 foot pole. There are three 25 foot flag poles on either side of Old Glory with 3' x 5' Navy, Marine, and Coast Guard flags on one side and Army, Air Force, and POW/MIA flags on the other side. In between are three 6 foot statues of saluting soldiers representing Marine, Army, and Navy.

There is a 6' x 3' granite marker with my poem, A Soldiers Lament, laser engraved on one side and a picture of a huey gun ship hovering over elephant grass with a squad of infantry men jumping into a hot LZ on the other side. There is a granite plaque with all the statistics of Vietnam war KIA/MIA on the front side and a field cross with an M-16, a fixed bayonet, a helmet and boots. Another plaque has a sculpture of the Medal of Honor with the names of the men in my unit who received the honor engraved in the granite.

There are three granite benches to sit and meditate on and every day I have vets who come by and do that. I also

sit and remember my buddies who were with me and all those from all the wars this Country has participated in for our freedom. I say a prayer for them. I'm proud to be an American.

As I sit and meditate my mind goes back to Vietnam. I see jet fighters dropping napalm. I see B-52 bombers dropping 500lb bombs. I see gunships, Gatling guns, and "Puff the Magic Dragon." I see North Vietnamese charging in human wave attacks and I can see my buddies so young and so brave fighting with valor and courage. I see bodies laying all over the battle field.

I can see my friends in the clouds. I can see angels singing and the Gates of Heaven open as they enter, standing tall in formation. I can see God with a big, white robe spread open. He wraps his robe around them and holds them to His bosom and I feel so much emotion. Tears stream down my face. They look so perfect and their faces are so happy. I love my friends and I hope and pray that someday I will qualify to be with them in heaven, standing with them in formation in the bosom of our Lord for all eternity.

My life has been blessed and all the success and glory go to Jesus Christ, my Lord and Savior.

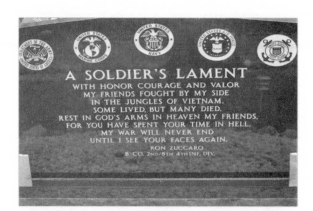

A SOLDIER'S LAMENT

WITH HONOR COURAGE AND VALOR
MY FRIENDS FOUGHT BY MY SIDE
IN THE JUNGLES OF VIETNAM.
SOME LIVED, BUT MANY DIED.
REST IN GOD'S ARMS IN HEAVEN MY FRIENDS,
FOR YOU HAVE SPENT YOUR TIME IN HELL.
MY WAR WILL NEVER END
UNTIL I SEE YOUR FACES AGAIN.

RON ZUCCARO
B. CO. 2ND/8TH 4TH INF. DIV.

1962 - 1975

SMITH
ELMENLINDO R. S/SGT
WILLETT
LOUIS E. PFC
ROARK
ANUND C. SGT
MOLNAR
FRANK Z. S/SGT
McMERNEY
DAVID H. 1/SGT
McDONALD
PHILL G. PFC
JOHNSON
DWIGHT H. SP/5
EVANS
DONALD W. JR. SP/4
GRANDSTAFF
BRUCE ALAN P/SGT
BENNETT
THOMAS W. CPL
BELLRICHARD
LESLIE ALLEN PFC